The
Great Depression
and World War II

The Great Depression and World War II

Tanya Lee Stone

RAINTREE
STECK-VAUGHN
PUBLISHERS

A Harcourt Company

Austin · New York
www.steck-vaughn.com

For my Dad, A. Harris, who taught me that you can only write one good sentence at a time.

Published by Raintree Steck-Vaughn Publishers, an imprint of Steck-Vaughn Company

Developed by Discovery Books
Editor: Sabrina Crewe
Designer: Sabine Beaupré
Maps: Stefan Chabluk

Raintree Steck-Vaughn Publishers Staff
Publishing Director: Walter Kossmann
Art Director: Max Brinkmann
Editor: Shirley Shalit

Consultant Andrew Frank, California State University, Los Angeles

Library of Congress Cataloging-in-Publication Data
Stone, Tanya Lee
    The Great Depression and World War II / Tanya Lee Stone.
        p. cm. -- (The making of America)
    Includes bibliographical references and index.
    ISBN 0-8172-5710-1
    1. United States--History--1933-1945--Juvenile literature. 2. United States--History--1919-1933--Juvenile literature. 3. Depressions--1929--United States--Juvenile literature. 4. World War, 1939-1945--Causes--Juvenile literature. 5. World War, 1939-1945--United States--Juvenile literature. [1. United States--History--1933-1945. 2. United States--History--1919-1933. 3. Depressions--1929. 4. World War, 1939-1945--United States.] I. Title. II. Making of America (Austin, Tex.)

E806 .S818 2001
973.91--dc21

                                                                00-059168

Printed and bound in the United States of America
1 2 3 4 5 6 7 8 9 0   IP   04 03 02 01 00

Acknowledgments
Cover The Granger Collection; p. 8 Corbis; p. 10 The Granger Collection; pp. 11, 13, 15, 19, 20, 21, 22, 23, 24, 26, 30, 32, 34, 35, 36, 42, 45, 47, 48, 50, 51, 54 Corbis; p. 55 Milwaukee County Historical Society; pp. 56, 57, 58, 61, 62, 64, 65, 66, 68, 71, 72 Corbis; p. 73 The Granger Collection; pp. 75, 76, 79, 80, 81, 83, 84, 85 Corbis.

Cover illustration: The Japanese attacked Pearl Harbor, Hawaii, on December 7, 1941, bringing the United States into World War II. This photograph shows three U.S. battleships: (from left to right) the *West Virginia*, the *Tennessee*, and the *Arizona*. The first two were damaged in the attack, and the *Arizona* was sunk.

Contents

Introduction

In the 1920s, America was experiencing a boom. World War I was over and people were enjoying life. The decade is often referred to as the "Roaring Twenties." The period of Prohibition, when the sale of alcohol was forbidden, sparked a rebellious outpouring of excess. People went to illegal nightclubs to drink and dance and listen to music. The Jazz Age was born during the 1920s, bringing with it explosive music from artists such as Louis Armstrong and Bessie Smith.

Technology was advancing at a fast pace and Americans were enjoying radio, magazines, and modern appliances. Unemployment was down. President Herbert Hoover was confident that the economy would remain healthy. It seemed that America was on a smooth road with no bumps in sight.

However, the stock market crash of 1929 changed everything. The nation was thrown into the depths of an economic depression. For 12 years, despite reform programs and bouts of recovery, the American economy suffered. The Great Depression did not lift until the United States was pulled into the huge conflict of World War II, in which Americans fought on the battlefields of Europe, North Africa, and the islands of the Pacific.

World War II brought other changes to the nation. America was transformed from a country that believed in isolationism, or staying out of foreign affairs, to one that intervened in a foreign war. Men were sent overseas to fight, and women and minorities took their places in the workforce. World War II changed America's destiny forever.

The Roaring Twenties Screech to a Halt

The country's economy seemed to be in excellent shape. Most people assumed that things would stay the way they were for some time. They poured their money into the stock market in the hope of becoming rich.

The Crash of 1929

During the 1920s, the stock market had become an extremely popular way to make money. People invested their dollars in stock, which means they bought shares of a particular company, many borrowing money to do so. The object of investing in the stock market is to buy shares at a low price and sell them later for a higher price. As the companies that Americans were investing in prospered, their shares increased in value.

Stock prices rose at a fast pace throughout 1927, 1928, and into the summer of 1929. The rate at which individuals, banks, and companies bought shares during the summer of 1929 was so high that it pushed up the prices artificially. It was the demand to buy shares rather than the actual success of companies that was causing the prices to rise. This meant the value of a specific stock was not related to anything real.

By 1929, banks had loaned almost $6 billion to people buying shares. With such a large amount of money being loaned, a dramatic decrease in the value of the stock market would have a drastic effect. In the fall of 1929, people felt

"I am firm in my belief that anyone not only can be rich, but ought to be rich."

John J. Raskob, director of General Motors, before the stock market crash of 1929

that the tremendous upswing couldn't last much longer. Many got nervous and decided to sell their shares. But when most people sell and very few buy, the system "crashes." That is what happened in October 1929.

On October 24, there was a crisis. Almost 13 million shares were exchanged, an enormous number at that time. On the following Tuesday, October 29, nearly 16 million shares were sold. Because of this heavy sell-off, people panicked, prices plummeted, and the market crashed.

The Empire State Building

As America sank into depression, a leftover symbol of the Roaring Twenties rose up in New York City. Lack of space in fast-growing cities had led to the construction of higher and higher buildings to accommodate the expanding population. The Empire State Building, designed by architect William Lamb, was the most ambitious skyscraper yet.

Amazingly, the Empire State Building took only one year and 45 days to build. An average workforce of 2,500 people a day worked shifts around the clock. The building rose by about four and a half stories every week; but in one ten-day period, 14 floors were completed. When it was finished, the skyscraper stood 102 stories and 1,250 feet (381 m) high, towering above the New York skyline. Due to the Great Depression, the office building took ten years to fill with renters and earned itself the nickname of the "Empty State Building." Completed in 1931, the Empire State Building remained the tallest structure in the world for 41 years.

Many people and companies lost all they had. Those who had borrowed money to buy shares also fell deeply in debt.

Causes of Depression

The stock market crash of 1929 was the beginning of a period in American history called the Great Depression. There had been other indications that hard times were in store for Americans. Two of these were the falling sales of automobiles and new homes. In fact, the rate at which new homes were being built had slowed considerably by the mid-1920s. This was significant at a time when the economy was supposedly strong and housing was needed.

But was the economy really strong? It was true that the United States had experienced a post-war boom after World War I, and that technology was rapidly advancing. American companies produced modern conveniences such as radios, phonographs, canned and frozen foods, and electric kitchen appliances. With more workers needed to increase production, employment rates went up.

Even though the size of the middle class grew during the 1920s, workers' salaries did not increase much. It was clear that there was an unequal distribution of wealth in the country. The families who had grown truly rich in the boom were in a minority, and the nation was more prosperous in appearance than in reality.

The country's banking system was not as sound as it might have been. There were too many independent banks and not enough rules to keep people's money safe should something go wrong with the economy. If people withdraw all of their money from a particular bank, it causes what is called a "run" on that bank. And if the public has lost faith in the banking system, as it had in 1929, a run on one bank often leads to the same thing occurring at other banks. In 1929, more than 650 banks had to close. In 1930, that number grew to 1,352.

Another cause of the Depression was the economic consequence of World War I in Europe. The defeated nation of Germany owed vast sums of money to other, victorious

"There is not an unemployed man in the country that hasn't contributed to the wealth of every millionaire in America."

Comic Will Rogers, November 1931

European countries, especially Britain and France. Those two nations, in turn, owed the United States $10 billion and were not able to pay it. The American economy, already struggling with financial problems, had to manage without repayments of this huge debt.

"Brother, Can You Spare a Dime?"

The stock market crash had a rapid and terrible effect on employment. In the early days of the Depression, there were no government programs to offer financial help to people who lost their jobs. It wasn't until 1932 that President Hoover authorized the government to spend federal money to help the unemployed.

In some instances, factories were shut down overnight. In others, production decreased dramatically, wages were cut, and jobs were lost. Since employers everywhere were in trouble, once a person lost a job it was extremely difficult to find another one. Some factories tried to keep going and not cut jobs, instead shortening workdays to reduce the amount of money spent on wages. In 1929, more than 1.5 million people were unemployed. That number grew to more than 12 million by 1932, an increase of more than 600 percent in just three years. In 1933, one in four American workers was out of a job.

During the Depression, widespread unemployment caused homelessness and hunger in America. People who had recently been homeowners with good jobs found themselves in line at soup kitchens, such as this one in New York City in 1931.

By 1932, it was no longer just factory workers who made up the unemployed. Experienced engineers, skilled laborers, teachers, and other professionals often had to find creative ways of making a few dollars. Some sold apples on the street, while others shined shoes to make ends meet.

One popular song called "Brother, Can You Spare a Dime?" summed up the situation in which many people found themselves. They lost not only their jobs but their homes too, as banks called in their loans. With people desperate for shelter, shantytowns—clusters of makeshift shacks—sprang up.

Hoovervilles

People who lost their homes in the Depression had nowhere to go and no money to spend. They began to build makeshift shelters from cardboard, scrap metal, canvas, wood, paper, and other discarded materials that they found at city dumps. Clusters of these shelters sprang up on vacant ground in cities, forming shantytowns that became known as "Hoovervilles." They were named for President Hoover, who was blamed by many Americans for the poverty of the Depression.

A large Hooverville sprawls across an empty lot in Seattle, Washington, in 1934.

Residents of Hoovervilles lived in insanitary and depressing conditions. There was no plumbing, clean water, or adequate food. Sickness and disease spread rapidly, and both adults and children suffered from malnutrition. These shantytowns, found all over the country, became one of the saddest symbols of the Great Depression.

Lines of people wrapped around city blocks waiting for handouts of food from churches and private charities. Places such as the YMCA in New York City fed as many as 12,000 hungry people each day.

Farmers Dump Crops

Tragically, at the same time that thousands of people were going hungry, there was actually an abundance of food going to waste on America's farms. Crop prices were low in the 1920s and so farmers' incomes shrank. During the Depression, prices for crops and other products, such as meat and milk, dropped lower than the farmers' actual cost of growing and producing them.

Between 1929 and 1932, the price of wheat dropped by two-thirds. Drastic price slashing affected cotton, corn, and other farm products in the same period. Cotton, for example, went from 17 cents to 6 cents a pound, and corn went from 81 cents to 33 cents a bushel. Because of this, some farmers actually destroyed their crops because they could not afford to grow them. Dairy farmers dumped hundreds and hundreds of gallons of milk in protest at the low prices. But the prices just kept dropping.

It was often impossible for farmers to survive under these circumstances. Many could not make enough money to keep up with the cost of paying off their bank loans, and thousands lost their farms.

Minorities Suffer

Hunger, poverty, and homelessness were affecting a majority of Americans, but minority groups suffered the most. During the 1920s, while many white Americans had prospered, most African Americans had remained poor. And during the Great Depression, black workers were likely to be laid off before white workers. In addition, jobs that had been typically held by African Americans—such as those of elevator operators, waiters, maids, and trash collectors—were taken away from them and given to white people in need of work instead. By

1932, more than one-third of the nation's blacks were out of work. Even those who were able to keep their jobs often had to endure wage cuts of up to 50 percent. In the South, hard times led to intolerance. Violence toward blacks, which had decreased considerably since the turn of the century, rose again.

As the 1930s went on, there was growing sentiment that scarce jobs and food should only be given to "real" Americans. As a result, many Mexican Americans lost their jobs. In addition, almost 500,000 people were forcibly sent back to Mexico during the 1930s. Many reports indicate that nearly half of these people were U.S. citizens. Although the program was supposed to be voluntary, in practice it was not. People were rounded up and put on trains just for looking Mexican.

Global Repercussions

By the 1920s, the economies of nations all over the world had become intertwined. For example, workers in Southeast Asia produced rubber for car tires that would also require steel made in British or American steel mills. And countries such as Brazil, which grew coffee for export, depended on other nations buying their products. In this way, positive and negative economic trends in one country affected other countries.

African Americans in the South, such as this man and child in Alabama, did not experience a sharp change during the Great Depression. Most were already poor and many unemployed. Still, life became harder for African Americans than it had been. The handful who had owned land lost it and, if they were lucky, became laborers for white farmers.

The downward turn in the European and American economies during the Depression had a far-reaching impact. As exports all over the world decreased, production slowed down. Millions of jobs were lost worldwide, and unemployment in other nations hit between 15 percent and 25 percent of the workforce.

After World War I, the United States began to invest in railways and a wide variety of factories overseas. As these businesses failed during the Depression, people believed the U.S. economy was suffering from having been tangled up in international affairs. This made Americans even more committed to the idea of isolationism in the future.

President Hoover's Response

President Hoover believed strongly in the idea that people needed to take care of themselves or rely on neighbors and private charity for assistance in times of need. He referred to this concept as "rugged individualism." After all, America had been built on that idea since the pioneer days.

Hoover felt that welfare would lead to people being more interested in handouts than hard work. This was the way that the federal government had operated over the past century. But what Hoover failed to realize was that overcoming the crisis of the Great Depression was going to take new ways of thinking about government.

The president did, eventually, begin to see that the government had a role to play in easing the burden. In 1932, the Reconstruction Finance Corporation (RFC) was established by Hoover. It was created to give loans to banks and businesses, as well as to states for relief purposes. However, although Congress had up to $300 million to spend for relief, Hoover restricted the use of these funds.

Although he may always be remembered as an ineffective leader, Hoover played an important role in government. If he had been too quick to jump in and exert control, it is likely he would have met with opposition. Nevertheless, America was ready for new leadership.

> "The lesson should be constantly enforced that though the people support the government, the government should not support the people."
>
> *President Hoover, 1930*

Herbert Clark Hoover (1874–1964)

Herbert Hoover was born in Iowa and moved to Oregon in 1884 to live with his aunt and uncle after his parents died. In 1891, he went to study mining engineering at what is now Stanford University in California. As an engineer, Hoover traveled to Australia and China, and in 1908 opened his own engineering company.

During World War I, Hoover's efforts to help get food supplies to war-torn Belgium led to his appointment as the United States food administrator. In this position, he created programs to increase food production and improve distribution of available food during the war.

Hoover became secretary of commerce in 1921 and ran for president in 1928. The Great Depression hit during his first term. Because of his belief in individual independence, President Hoover was slow to institute any government relief programs during the Depression. Americans were angered by his apparent lack of wisdom and compassion. People blamed their dire situation on Hoover's lack of response and he lost the 1932 election to Franklin Delano Roosevelt. Hoover spent several years out of the spotlight. In the late 1940s and into the 1950s, however, he was a respected adviser in Washington, D.C.

Roosevelt is Elected

The Depression was in full swing during the presidential election of 1932. The Republican party nominated President Hoover for reelection, but he didn't appear to have much of a chance. The Democrats nominated Franklin Delano Roosevelt (FDR), the governor of New York, as their presidential candidate. It was no surprise when FDR won by a landslide.

Roosevelt's confidence and charm were exactly what the American people needed. In his famous inaugural address on March 4, 1933, his reassuring words were, "This great nation will endure as it has endured, will revive and will prosper."

Economic Depression in the United States

The Great Depression was not the only economic crisis the United States has endured. There were depressions throughout the seventeenth, eighteenth, and the nineteenth centuries. America's first major banking crisis, in 1819, sent the nation into a depression for three years.

The activity created by war has helped the economy of the United States on more than one occasion. Both the American Revolution and the War of 1812 created "war booms." America's economy boomed during and after World War I, except for a recession in 1920 and 1921. And it took the huge industrial output during World War II finally to end the Great Depression.

In the 1970s, after a period of growth in America's economy since World War II, the country slowed down again. The cost of living—basic expenses such as housing and food—rose, and so did levels of unemployment. In 1981 and 1982, unemployment climbed over 10 percent and wages dropped sharply.

As the country recovered in the mid-1980s, inflation and a soaring trade on the stock market led to a "crash" in 1987, similar to but not as severe as the one of 1929. But this time, a depression did not result. Lessons had been learned from the Great Depression, and the economy was saved from a crisis, mostly because government poured money into the banking system to stabilize the stock market.

Roosevelt Takes Control

President Roosevelt took immediate action to strengthen the economy and morale of the United States. America was looking for a strong leader and that is exactly what it got. The new president wasted no time in introducing a flurry of legislation, known as Roosevelt's "New Deal," to address the problems of the time.

> "We are going to make a country in which no one is left out."
>
> *President Roosevelt during his first term, to Secretary of Labor Frances Perkins*

The First 100 Days

In the month before Roosevelt's inauguration, the nation's banking system went from bad to worse. The day after he was sworn in on March 4, 1933, Roosevelt declared a four-day bank holiday. This gave banks and Congress time to inspect the state of the banking system and create emergency banking laws to avert further crisis. The action inspired Americans to put their trust, and money, back into the banks, and deposits soon exceeded withdrawals.

On March 9, President Roosevelt signed the Emergency Banking Relief Act. By June, an existing banking act, the Glass-Steagall Act, was improved. The most important new component of this act was the creation of the Federal Deposit Insurance Corporation (FDIC). This offered federal insurance to guarantee people's deposits. The idea made many people nervous, but it turned out to be a success.

Roosevelt also quickly gave the Reconstruction Finance Corporation (RFC) new life. The RFC had been established by Hoover in 1932, but it had not loaned out enough money to achieve its goals. In addition to this, on May 12 another agency, the Federal Emergency Relief Administration

Franklin Delano Roosevelt (1882–1945) and Eleanor Roosevelt (1884–1962)

Franklin Delano Roosevelt (FDR) was the only American president ever to be elected to office for four terms. He was a man of incomparable spirit and strength who led the United States through two crises: the Great Depression and World War II.

FDR was born in Hyde Park, New York, into a wealthy New York family. He trained and practiced as a lawyer in New York, where he was also a state senator from 1911 to 1913. In 1913, Roosevelt became assistant secretary of the United States Navy. In 1920, he was chosen to run for vice president with the Democratic presidential candidate, James M. Cox. However, Cox and Roosevelt were defeated in the election by the Republicans. The next year, FDR became very ill with the disease of polio. As a result, he had limited use of his legs and was disabled for the remainder of his life.

In 1928, Roosevelt was elected governor of New York. At the start of the Great Depression, FDR's reforms brought some needed relief to the state. He was reelected as New York's governor by a landslide in 1930, and again received a huge vote when he was elected president of the United States in 1932.

As president, Roosevelt had a profound effect on American history. He introduced major changes with his New Deal legislation and proved to be a strong and confident leader during World War II. Roosevelt died on April 12, 1945, before he was able to witness the end of the war.

Like her husband, Eleanor Roosevelt was born into a well-to-do New York family. She was a distant cousin of FDR, whom she married in 1905, and a niece of former president Theodore Roosevelt. Although shy, Eleanor Roosevelt was an intelligent and strong woman. From the time that her husband became disabled by polio, she was determined to help him remain active. By the time she became first lady, Eleanor Roosevelt had a reputation as a political figure to be respected. She served as the president's ambassador and traveled the world on his behalf. Eleanor Roosevelt was a champion of the underprivileged in American society and actively supported civil rights for minorities until her death.

(FERA), was created to give money to states to help with the unemployed.

Providing relief to the farmers of America and increasing crop prices was also a high priority. In May 1933, the Agriculture Adjustment Act (AAA) was passed. Farmers were paid to reduce their land use, given help with loans, and guaranteed minimum prices for certain produce. The idea was to create a shortage, which would lead to higher demand, and thus drive up crop prices. The AAA did not make a swift and dramatic difference, but it helped ease the burden on farmers at a critical time.

In June 1933, the National Recovery Administration (NRA) was formed. Its purpose was to revive industry and reduce unemployment. It also set basic rights for workers regarding wages and working conditions. The Public Works Administration (PWA) was another weapon against the Depression. It created projects that provided jobs and stimulated the economy. New York's Lincoln Tunnel and Triborough Bridge were constructed under this program, and so were the Bonneville and Grand Coulee Dams on the Columbia River in Washington. Many hospitals, libraries, and municipal buildings were built through the PWA. The creation of the Civilian Conservation Corps (CCC) allowed young people the opportunity to find work restoring the country's forests and parks. They planted trees and built roads, trails, and campgrounds.

In addition to persuading Congress to pass all this legislation, Roosevelt made another move that endeared him to the American people. He legalized the sale of beer, which led to the end of Prohibition in 1933.

One of President Roosevelt's popular moves was the introduction of his famous "Fireside Chats." The president used the radio, which had a large and growing audience, to explain his policies to the American public. He wanted to boost American morale, and people were reassured and comforted by this window into the workings of their government.

Rebuilding Begins

Parts of the New Deal worked, while others fell short. In the spring of 1934, there was still a lot of damage to repair before the economy could be considered healthy.

All over America, people labored on public projects under the WPA program. The WPA sign, displayed by this street-widening project, became a familiar sight.

The Works Progress Administration (WPA) was set up in 1935 to provide millions of temporary jobs such as building or improving schools, hospitals, playgrounds, and airports. Writers, artists, actors, and musicians also found employment through the WPA's cultural programs. The WPA offered people alternatives to the humiliation of receiving financial handouts from the government. Its intentions were good, but there were difficulties. The government did not want to make the WPA programs so attractive that they discouraged people from finding private employment. Because of this, the WPA usually offered very low wages and little job security.

Two other important New Deal programs helped rebuild the economy and morale of the country. In June 1934, the Securities and Exchange Commission was set up to make sure the stock market operated fairly and honestly. The Social Security Act was established in 1935 to provide unemployment benefits and funds for people once they stopped working after the age of 65. It also provided aid for people with disabilities and for mothers and children in need.

The Dust Bowl

In the 1930s, parts of the United States experienced a terrible blow from nature in addition to the economic crisis of the Great Depression. Dry and dusty winds began in 1933 to blow across Texas and Oklahoma and lasted for several years. In 1934, windstorms went on to ravage a region of America that stretched from Missouri and Arkansas through Oklahoma, Kansas, and Texas to New Mexico and Colorado. The region generally receives little rainfall, and a drought from 1934 to 1937 left the land with poor resistance to the wind. The dry dirt was simply blown away. This vast area of the Midwest became known as the "Dust Bowl."

Farms throughout the Dust Bowl region were devastated and families had no choice but to pack up and leave, abandoning their homes and livelihoods. With their cars piled to the roof with children, pets, and possessions, people took to the road in search of new lives and ways to earn a living.

Large numbers of migrant families from Oklahoma traveled to California in search of work. There, many of them lived in farm labor camps until they found jobs. At one camp, the Weedpatch near Bakersfield, California, children and teachers built their own school. Author John Steinbeck wrote about the Weedpatch camp and the Great Depression years in his famous novel *The Grapes of Wrath*.

A Dust Bowl farm stands abandoned, just a year after the start of the terrible winds.

Minorities and the New Deal

Unfortunately, there were few New Deal improvements geared specifically to the African American population. Roosevelt needed the support of the entire Congress, and felt that a focus on the plight of blacks would lose him the crucial support of Southern congressmen.

Discrimination against African Americans often resulted in unfair distribution of relief funds. In some cases, white recipients were paid 70 percent more than black recipients. And where NRA regulations called for equal pay regardless of race, many black workers lost their jobs to make room for white workers.

Nevertheless, certain improvements were made for African Americans. Up to 20 percent of WPA workers were black, and Roosevelt banned racial discrimination on WPA projects. In addition, the minimum wage that was paid by the WPA was significantly more than many African Americans had made in the past. Literacy programs were also put into place by the WPA. Nearly 25 percent of people who were taught to read through these programs were black.

African American voters showed their loyalty to President Roosevelt. Historically, the majority of blacks had voted Republican since it was the Republican Abraham Lincoln and his Emancipation Proclamation that had spelled the end of slavery in America. This political loyalty to the Republican party remained until Roosevelt took strides to make life better for the black population through New Deal programs. The Democratic party began to win the black vote and 76 percent of black voters, mainly from the North, voted for FDR in the 1936 election.

President Roosevelt placed more than 130 African Americans in federal positions between 1933 and 1940.

In 1937, Roosevelt appointed William Hastie to a district court in the U.S. Virgin Islands. Hastie (left) is shown here taking his oath of office in 1949 as the first black federal judge of a United States Circuit Court of Appeals.

Mary McLeod Bethune (1875–1955)

Mary McLeod Bethune was born in Mayesville, South Carolina, the youngest of 17 children. Her parents were former slaves who believed strongly in the power of education. Because of this, their daughter was able to attend school and go on to college at the Moody Bible Institute in Chicago. After teaching in Georgia, Bethune founded the Daytona Normal and Industrial Institute for Negro Girls in Daytona, Florida, in 1904. The school was very successful and Bethune merged it with Cookman, a boy's school, in 1925. She became known as a pioneer in black education and caught the attention of white political leaders all over the country.

Mary McLeod Bethune (left) listens to a speech by Eleanor Roosevelt.

Bethune was an extremely important influence on Eleanor Roosevelt's thinking about racial issues and the problems facing black Americans. The first lady helped Bethune become director of the Division of Negro Affairs of the National Youth Administration. Bethune said of the government's new attitudes, "Never before in the history of America has Negro youth been offered such opportunities." Bethune was also involved in other New Deal government agencies. In addition, she founded the National Council of Negro Women and was a vice president of the National Association for the Advancement of Colored People (NAACP).

These officials often gathered to discuss issues and became known as the "black cabinet." The president also appointed several white Supreme Court justices who were known supporters of racial equality.

Trouble with the Supreme Court

There was, of course, opposition to all of the sweeping changes that Roosevelt was bringing about. FDR's approach to government was radical: Federal relief and the idea of welfare were, after all, entirely new ideas. Many disagreed with the president's aims for the nation. Most of all, they were worried by his inclination to expand the role of the federal government.

Roosevelt's new "liberal" approach often met with opposition from big business owners who thought it would threaten their profits and ability to control their businesses. Others disliked Roosevelt's ideas for political reasons: They saw them as a move toward socialism, which is an economic system based on government ownership and regulation of a nation's production.

The NRA symbol, a blue eagle, was displayed by businesses who adopted NRA standards for their workers. It became such a patriotic symbol that the newly formed Philadelphia Eagles football team took its name from the NRA bird. However, following the Supeme Court's ruling on NIRA in 1935, the NRA blue eagle ceased to fly.

The U.S. Supreme Court also opposed some of the New Deal programs. New Dealers had hoped that the Court would see the emergency of the Great Depression as a good reason to extend many governmental powers. For a time, the Court did. But in 1935, it used its powers to overturn the National Industrial Recovery Act (NIRA). This law, passsed in 1933, had created the NRA and the PWA. The Supreme Court declared NIRA to be unconstitutional because it gave the president the power to regulate business practices.

In 1936, the Supreme Court also questioned actions of the AAA and declared some of its practices unconstitutional. And in June 1936, the Court declared New York's minimum wage unconstitutional. People on many political fronts were angered by this ruling. Even Supreme Court Justice Harlan Stone wrote of the decision, "We finished the term of Court yesterday, I think in many ways one of the most disastrous in history."

By 1937, Roosevelt was worried about the direction in which the Court seemed to be heading. Over the next few years, five of the nine positions on the Supreme Court became vacant and Roosevelt filled them with more liberal justices. The new group was referred to as the "Roosevelt Court" because it supported New Deal policies and was willing to give the federal government the power to improve the American economy.

The Growth of the Labor Movement

It was not just the government that wanted to establish fair wages and conditions for workers. Automobile, rubber, and steel industry workers were increasingly angered by the way they were treated. Industrial workers began to fight for their own rights. Sit-down strikes became commonplace across the country. A strike occurs when employees refuse to work until their demands for higher wages or better working conditions are met. In a sit-down strike, workers would literally sit down inside the workplace so that the company could not use other workers to keep the factory machinery running.

In the first four months of 1937, sit-down strikes were held at major American companies: General Motors, Ford, Chrysler, Buick, and Republic Steel. These strikes led to violence in some instances. In January 1937, a strike by automobile workers in Flint, Michigan, held after a sit-down protest ten days earlier, quickly turned violent. No lives were lost, but guns and other weapons, such as thrown rocks and bottles, seriously injured more than 20 people. Ultimately, the strikes in Michigan led to a settlement that gave the workers much of what they wanted. This encouraged workers in other industries to follow the example of the workers in Flint.

"We don't want violence. We just want to protect our husbands and we are going to."

Wife of striker in Flint, Michigan, 1937

25

It was not only in manufacturing but also in service industries that working people campaigned for better conditions. These cheerful dime store employees took part in a sit-down strike in 1937. They appealed for the public to support them in their demand for a 40-hour working week. At the time, their employers could set working hours according to their own needs rather than those of their workers.

Labor Unions Take Action

The sit-down strike technique did not just spring out of random tactics developed by workers. Workers joined together in labor unions that supported and organized the fight for their rights. One such organization, the American Federation of Labor (AFL), focused on skilled workers in trades such as carpentry and electrical work.

At the AFL's annual meeting in October 1935, John L. Lewis, president of the United Mine Workers, spoke out in favor of unions for unskilled workers, those who worked as laborers in industry. A few weeks later, the Committee for Industrial Organization (CIO) was created within the AFL. It was soon renamed the Congress of Industrial Organizations and became independent of the AFL.

From 1936 on, the CIO had great success in organizing industrial workers. Their sit-down strikes spread from the auto and steel industries to shipbuilding yards, oil refineries, rubber plants, and textile mills.

Even with these successes, the road ahead was rocky. A victory for steel workers was achieved when U.S. Steel signed an agreement with the CIO in March 1937, but many other companies would not accept unionization. These included Ford Motor Company, Goodyear Rubber, and Republic Steel. A disastrous event on May 30, 1937, fueled the conflict between labor unions and management. A group of union demonstrators at a Republic Steel mill in Chicago was fired on by police. During the event, known as the Memorial Day Massacre, ten people were killed and 84 injured.

After the Memorial Day Massacre, the demands for labor unionization lost some steam. There were several reasons for this. Many middle-class Americans, while they were in favor of fair conditions and pay, did not agree with some of the violent methods used to obtain union goals. And just when America seemed to be safely coming out of the Depression, the nation suffered another recession. In addition, the U.S. Supreme Court ruled in 1939 that sit-down strikes were illegal. Only the war that loomed ahead would provide the motive for companies and unions to work together.

Social Security and Welfare

Federal assistance for individuals did exist before 1935. In 1862, the government made funds available to soldiers who had been disabled in the Civil War and, in 1906, extended them to include elderly veterans. From the 1920s on, U.S. government employees could depend on retirement and disability money.

However, the Social Security Act, passed in 1935 and still in place today, was a dramatic change because it affected a much larger group of citizens. It provided funds to business or industry workers when they retired. Both workers and employers contributed to the funds. The act was soon amended to include the families of retired or deceased workers. It was expanded again in 1950 to include workers in many fields other than business or industry. By 1956, the Social Security Act applied to almost all workers in America.

Since the 1930s, a major transformation developed in the way Americans think about financial assistance from the government, or welfare. Before the act passed, it was simply a fact of life that Americans needed to provide for themselves without any help. But that way of thinking has gradually changed. Today, welfare comes in many forms. There is help available for training and education, for unemployment and disability, healthcare, and for families living in severe poverty. Americans have come to depend on the financial help that welfare provides. As the welfare system grows, however, so does the debate about how beneficial it really is to society. Some people believe that, instead of providing a safety net for the most disadvantaged, welfare discourages poorer people from helping themselves.

War Breaks Out

In the early 1930s, dark forces were at work abroad. Dictators (rulers who take absolute control of a nation and are supported by military forces) came into power in Germany, Italy, Spain, and the Soviet Union. Japan was using military force to enhance its powers. Some of the world's leaders wanted to gain territory by using aggression. Others were focused, in addition, on ideas of racial purity and prejudice.

In the United States, there was a strong feeling that the nation should remain neutral. Americans had witnessed the complications of involvement in World War I and felt as though their country had taken on the burden of problems created by Europe. They wanted to remain isolated from what they saw as overseas disputes.

Economic Troubles After World War I

In 1919, at the end of World War I, the Treaty of Versailles was signed by Germany, France, Britain, and Italy. The U.S. Senate did not agree to the treaty's terms and America did not sign it. The Treaty of Versailles formally assigned the blame of World War I to Germany. It called for the size of the German army and navy to be reduced and imposed several territorial changes. The treaty also required that Germany make reparations, or payments for war damage and losses, to other countries.

In 1923, the German economy collapsed under the financial burden of reparations, weakening the entire European economy. This, in turn, had a negative effect

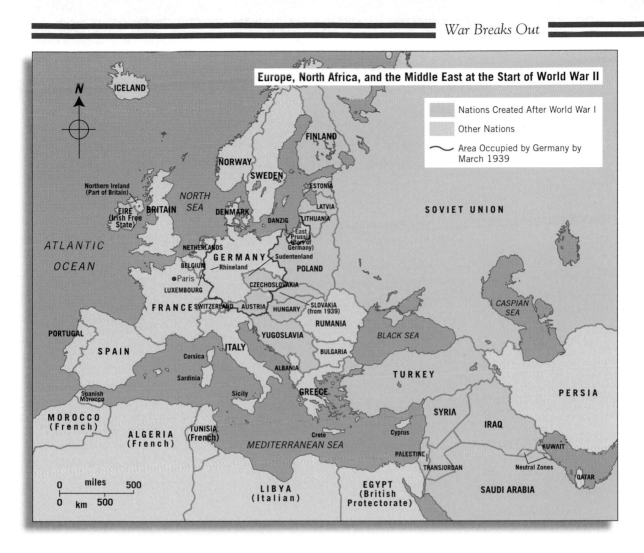

on the American economy. Britain and France had debts to the United States of about $10 billion and could not afford to pay them without the income expected from Germany. In order to solve this problem, a committee was formed in 1924 to stabilize the German economy and set up a system of gradual payments to Britain and France. The American banker and politician Charles G. Dawes was the committee's chairman, and his Dawes Plan put off the immediate crisis.

In May 1931, a banking crisis in Austria caused a panic. Many German banks closed, triggering a similar chain of events in neighboring European countries. The panic in Germany, along with financial troubles in Britain, dealt a

The Versailles Treaty at the end of World War I established new boundaries in Europe, and new nations came into existence. The Germans, humiliated by their defeat in the war, were not satisfied. By March 1939, Germany was fast encroaching on other countries.

hard blow to the struggling American economy. By the end of 1931, there were almost twice as many American bank closings as there had been in 1930. In 1931, President Hoover suspended foreign debts for one year in an effort to stop the destructive global financial cycle. This put an end to both reparations and war debt repayments, since the payments were never resumed.

Dictators in Western Europe

About the same time that Americans were welcoming Roosevelt into office, a new chancellor, Adolf Hitler, was taking power in Germany. Hitler had helped create the National Socialist German Workers', or Nazi, party in 1920. The Nazis were fascists, which means they believed in a powerful government with complete control over society and the economy. Nazis believed also that their race and nation were more important than individual rights, and they persecuted minority groups, such as Jews and gypsies. With Germany's economy in trouble and a depression setting in worldwide, Hitler was poised to take advantage of the German desire for strong leadership. Thousands of Germans supported his racist policies.

A huge crowd of soldiers in combat gear stands at attention to listen to Adolf Hitler speaking at a Nazi party rally in Nuremberg, Germany, in 1936. The Nazis held rallies during the 1930s both to display their military strength and to gain support in the country. The Nazi swastika symbol, seen on three large flags in the background, was displayed everywhere in Germany when the Nazis were at the height of their power.

One of Hitler's first actions as chancellor was to remove Germany from the League of Nations, set up after World War I to maintain peace. Hitler told the German people that they were not to blame for World War I, that the Treaty of Versailles was humiliating to their nation, and that the reparations were absolutely unfair. He also began to defy certain provisions of Versailles: In 1935, he began recruiting soldiers, and in 1936 he sent troops into the Rhineland, a part of Germany bordering France. Both of these actions had been forbidden by the treaty, but they went unchallenged.

This boldness made an impression on another fascist, the Italian dictator Benito Mussolini. Mussolini had seized power in 1922 and was the leader of Italy's Fascist party. In October 1935, Mussolini sent troops into Ethiopia to gain African territory for Italy. By May 1936, Italy had conquered Ethiopia, and the League of Nations had taken no action.

In addition to the activities of Hitler and Mussolini, the Spanish general Francisco Franco led a revolt against the legal government in Spain. Germany and Italy supported Franco throughout 1936 and 1937, and the fascist revolt against the Spanish government succeeded.

Hitler's Aggression Begins

Hitler then chose his next target. In March 1938, German troops took over Austria, forcing its chancellor to resign. In September of that same year, Hitler set his sights on Czechoslovakia, a democratic country that had been created by the Treaty of Versailles. Many of its citizens living in an area called the Sudetenland were originally German. Hitler demanded that the region be turned over to Germany. In 1939, he took the rest of Czechoslovakia. Although they objected to this move, Britain and France did not take action to protect that small nation. They hoped Hitler would now be satisfied and peace would be secured. They were mistaken.

A clear sign that Hitler was not about to be stopped was his violent persecution of Jewish people. Beginning in 1935, the Nuremberg Laws took away many rights of Jewish citizens

"History proves that dictatorships do not grow out of strong and successful governments, but out of weak and helpless ones."

President Roosevelt, in a "Fireside Chat," April 14, 1938

Ein Volk, ein Reich, ein Führer!

A poster of Adolf Hitler. The German slogan underneath means, "One people, one empire, one leader!"

Adolf Hitler (1889–1945)

Adolf Hitler was born in Austria. He moved to the Austrian capital Vienna after finishing school, hoping to be an artist, but he was not admitted to the art academy there. In 1913, Hitler moved to Munich, Germany. When World War I began, he enlisted in the German army. After the war, Hitler joined the German Workers' party in 1919, which he soon renamed the National Socialist German Workers' party, or Nazi party. Over the next two years, Hitler became the party's leader and ran it as a dictatorship. His long-term goals were to overthrow the current government and rid the nation of minorities that he deemed "undesirable." Despite a few setbacks in Hitler's career, one of which was a nine-month prison sentence after a failed attempt to overthrow the government, Germany's President Hindenburg appointed Hitler as chancellor of Germany in 1933.

Almost immediately, Hitler established himself as the nation's dictator. He destroyed most of the remaining political parties, and the Nazi party became extremely powerful. When Hindenburg died in 1934, Hitler declared himself supreme ruler of Germany. He took Germany and the rest of the world into World War II, during which the Nazis committed horrible atrocities against humankind. Hitler ended his own life in 1945 after realizing Germany would not win the war.

in Germany. On November 9, 1938, more than 7,000 Jewish businesses were destroyed, over 1,000 synagogues were burned, and Jewish cemeteries, schools, and homes were robbed. This violent destruction was named *Kristallnacht*, meaning "the night of broken glass." The next morning, nearly 30,000 Jews were arrested.

The Situation in the Soviet Union

Joseph Stalin came to power in the Soviet Union in 1925 as the head of the communist government. The basic theory behind communism is that the people have common ownership of all resources and property and everyone works for the good of the whole community. For example, by 1930, Stalin had set up a system in which millions of small, privately owned farms became part of large, state-owned properties. Instead of working for themselves, farmers worked for the state. Roads, cities, and power stations were built by hardworking Sovies who endured appalling injustices.

Although Soviet policies transformed the nation into a major power, Stalin ran the Soviet Union using secret police and brutality against all who disagreed with him. He was among the most tyrannical dictators that country had known.

> "We are fifty or a hundred years behind the advanced countries. We must make good this distance in ten years. Either we do it, or they crush us."
>
> *Soviet leader Joseph Stalin, February 4, 1931*

Japanese Aggression

Meanwhile, in Japan, there had been a focus on expansion of power and territory since the early 1900s. On September 18, 1931, Japanese troops set off explosives on a railroad track in Manchuria, a region of China that bordered the Soviet Union and had important natural resources. The Japanese then accused the Chinese of the act, creating an excuse for Japan to invade Manchuria. In February 1932, Japan renamed the region Manchukuo and set up a government there. The League of Nations issued a formal criticism and Japan withdrew from the organization. This weak response from the League encouraged Hitler and Mussolini in their pursuit of power and control in Europe.

Japan then launched a major attack in an effort to take control of China. Troops fired on Chinese soldiers on July 7, 1937. In August, the Japanese invaded the Chinese city of Shanghai. By November, the city had been conquered. Later that year, more than 50,000 Japanese soldiers entered another Chinese city, Nanking. The troops used brute force and committed terrible acts of violence, killing thousands of civilians.

*The towns of Poland were
defenseless against the
German blitzkrieg. Here, the
citizens and fire brigade
of a small Polish village
make a hopeless attempt to
fight fire and damage caused
by a German air attack.*

Germany Invades Poland

With all of the power struggles brewing, it seemed only a
matter of time before the constant crises erupted into a full-
blown war. That is exactly what happened just after midnight
on September 1, 1939.

German aircraft screamed over Poland, dropping their
bombs and destroying the Polish aircraft still on the ground.
Several hours later, German troops marched into Poland on
three sides. In the first of the German blitzkriegs, meaning
"lightning wars," Germany quickly defeated the Poles. In
response to these events, Britain and France—known as the
Allied Powers, or Allies—declared on September 3 that they
were at war with Germany. With this, Europe was thrown
into World War II.

The previous year, after Germany's initial attack on
Czechoslovakia, Britain and France had asked the Soviet
Union to unite with them against Hitler. But it was too late:
Stalin had already made a secret agreement with Hitler,
signing a non-aggression pact on August 23, 1939. Not only

did the agreement state that they would not fight against each other, it also declared that they would conquer and divide Poland. On September 17, 1939, the Soviet Union moved in from the east. By October, Poland was split up between the two bullying forces.

Occupation of Europe

Although Germany and the Soviet Union had signed a pact, Hitler's rapid and fierce attack on Poland worried Stalin. To ensure the Soviets would get their "fair share," Stalin's army invaded Finland on November 30, 1939. The Finns fought hard, but surrendered on March 12, 1940, and signed a peace treaty with the Soviet Union. Stalin then pushed in the direction of the small Baltic countries of Lithuania, Latvia, and Estonia, which neighbored the Soviet Union along the Baltic Sea. The Soviet Union occupied all three by June 1940.

On April 9, 1940, the Nazis attacked and seized strategic port cities in Norway. On the same day, they conquered Denmark. One month later, on May 10, German blitzkrieg brought destruction to the Netherlands, Belgium, and Luxembourg. The Germans entered these countries, achieving success with overwhelming speed. Luxembourg fell immediately, the Netherlands surrendered on May 14, and Belgium surrendered on May 28.

Also on May 14, Hitler's troops plowed through thick forest to the north of the Maginot Line (see map on page 37), a system of border fortifications built by the French for protection after World War I. The French were unable to stop the onslaught. The Germans moved across France and entered the capital, Paris, on June 14, 1940.

Nazi troops parade through the Arc de Triomphe and down the Champs Elysée, one of the main streets in Paris, during the German occupation of France in 1940. The capture of France greatly increased the German hope of European domination, and Great Britain, an island just a few miles from the French coast, was now very vulnerable.

"The Battle of France is over. I expect that the Battle of Britain is about to begin."

British Prime Minister Winston Churchill, June 1940

A few days before, Italy had declared war on the Allies, and Mussolini joined forces with Germany against France. Together, Germany and Italy were called the Axis Powers. France fell to the Germans on June 17 and signed an armistice with both Germany and Italy. Germany occupied the northern part of France and a Nazi flag flew from the Eiffel Tower in Paris. The southern region became a separate nation called Vichy France, which was loyal to Germany. The Nazis had conquered Europe from Poland to the Atlantic Ocean. Britain was their next target.

Germany and Britain Do Battle

Britain had counted on assistance from France to defend itself against Germany. But now the British were left without backup. The Battle of Britain began on July 10, 1940. In July

A German bomber flies above the British capital, London, during a raid in July 1940. The Battle of Britain completely destroyed large areas of London and other British cities.

and August, the German airforce—the Luftwaffe—heavily bombed British ships and bases of the British Royal Air Force, hoping to destroy grounded planes. The Luftwaffe also attacked cities, factories, and shipyards. During the bombing raids, people would spend their nights in underground shelters, or hurry for cover when the warning sirens sounded. Many surfaced after a raid to find their homes in ruins.

However, Britain fought hard, and on August 25 shifted the focus of the fight by bombing Germany's capital Berlin. The Germans retaliated and the two nations fought fiercely until the end of October 1940, when Germany abandoned the air battle. Hitler gave up his plans for an invasion of Britain.

By 1940, the European map had been redrawn. The Axis powers, led by Germany, had taken over much of Europe, including several countries that sided with the Allies. Part of France and its colonies were under control of the Vichy government; the other part of France was occupied by the Nazis.

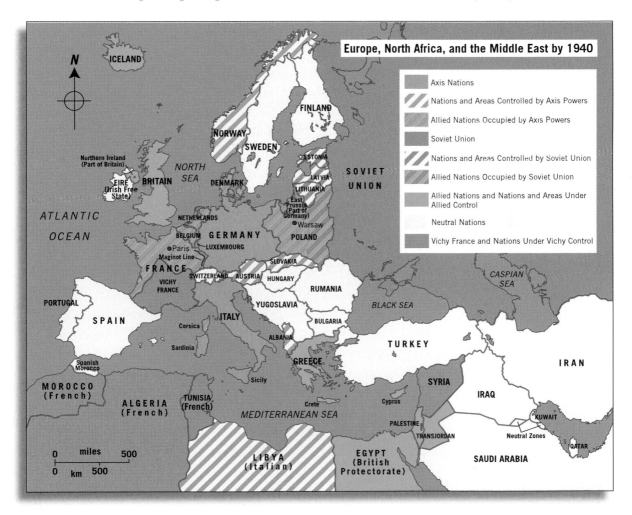

37

Japan Forms Alliance with Axis

Following the fall of France, the French colonies of Indochina (now Vietnam, Cambodia, and Laos) were vulnerable. The Japanese quickly tried to take control of Indochina, making an agreement with Vichy France to establish Japanese military bases there. On September 27, 1940, Japan signed the Tripartite Pact with Germany and Italy, becoming part of the Axis. With Japan on their side, the Axis Powers were now in a position to coax the United States out of isolationism with the threat of war in the Far East as well as war in Europe.

The United States tried to hinder Japan's aggression through economic means. Japan depended on the United States for important resources such as iron and steel. First, in October 1940, President Roosevelt banned the export of these products to all countries of the Eastern Hemisphere (the half of the world that includes Japan) except Britain. Next, when Japan occupied French Indochina in July 1941, all Japanese funds in America were temporarily seized by the federal government.

The American Climate

While all of these events were taking place on foreign soil, President Roosevelt had been occupied with the rebuilding of the United States' economy and morale. There was still a lot of work to be done to make the nation strong and vibrant once more.

The New Deal had done a lot to pull America out of the crisis of the Great Depression. When Roosevelt ran for reelection in 1936, he stressed the differences that his administration had made in the previous four years. The stock market seemed stable, industry had rallied, and construction of new homes and other buildings was up.

However, seven years after the crash of 1929, there were still more than 8 million unemployed. Many Americans felt the New Deal had run its course and lost its magic. Then, in 1937, just as President Roosevelt was turning his efforts to

Allied and Axis Powers During World War II

Allied Nations

As World War II progressed, more and more nations found it hard to remain neutral in the face of Axis aggression. By March 1945, all the countries below had joined the Allies.

Argentina	Australia	Belgium	Bolivia
Brazil	Britain	Canada	Chile
China	Colombia	Costa Rica	Cuba
Czechoslovakia	Denmark	Dominican Rep.	Ecuador
Egypt	El Salvador	Ethiopia	France
Greece	Guatemala	Haiti	Honduras
India	Iran	Iraq	Lebanon
Liberia	Luxembourg	Mexico	Mongolian
Netherlands	New Zealand	Nicaragua	People's Rep.
Norway	Panama	Paraguay	Peru
Poland	San Marino	Saudi Arabia	South Africa
Soviet Union	Syria	Turkey	United States
Uruguay	Venezuela	Yugoslavia	of America

Axis Nations

The countries below had all joined Germany to become Axis nations by the end of 1941. Vichy France, separated from German-occupied France in 1940, was also loyal to the Axis.

Albania	Bulgaria	Finland	Hungary
Italy	Japan	Rumania	Thailand

balancing the budget, there was another recession. The stock market hit another low and industrial production fell 33 percent. Another 2 million people lost their jobs.

American Opinion and Support

In this climate, Americans clung to isolationism. Debate grew about the increasing menace overseas, but most people wanted to focus on domestic issues and stay out of the war if possible. Neutrality Acts were passed in 1935, 1936, 1937, and 1939. These acts banned war materials from being sent to any nation at war. They prohibited loans to aggressive countries and warned Americans not to travel on any ship belonging to a nation at war.

During the Battle of Britain, British Prime Minister Winston Churchill, as he had done before, appealed to Roosevelt for aid. The president was gravely concerned about the fate of Europe but was committed to honoring his nation's desire to stay neutral. However, a concession was made with an agreement to send some American destroyers (small warships) to Britain. This occurred in an important trade with Britain called destroyers-for-bases, in which Britain gave America the use of naval bases in Bermuda, Newfoundland, the West Indies, and British Guiana in South America. This agreement brought America closer to an alliance with Britain.

As Roosevelt became more convinced that America would be pulled into the war, he set out both to inform and to rally the American people. Roosevelt wanted to be sure they understood the gravity of the situation and the role the United States needed to play. During a "Fireside Chat" radio broadcast on December 29, 1940, the president talked about the importance of supplying the Allies with the materials needed to wage a successful war.

"This nation will remain a neutral nation, but I cannot ask that every American remain neutral in thought as well."

President Roosevelt, in a "Fireside Chat," September 3, 1939

"We must be the great arsenal of democracy. For us this is an emergency as serious as war itself."

President Roosevelt, in a "Fireside Chat," December 29, 1940

Four Freedoms

On January 6, 1941, Roosevelt delivered his famous "Four Freedoms" speech. In it, he declared that, "In the future days, which we seek to make secure, we look forward to a world founded upon four essential human freedoms." He was referring to freedom of speech and expression, freedom of religion, freedom from want, and freedom from fear.

In March 1941, Congress passed Roosevelt's Lend-Lease Act. This allowed for greatly needed war materials to be sent to any country whose defense was important to the United

States. In spite of all of America's sound reasoning and declarations to remain neutral, it was difficult to avoid anti-Hitler feelings. By the time Roosevelt announced the Lend-Lease Act, the tide of popular opinion was turning.

Isolation or Intervention?

In both World War I and World War II, the United States was reluctant to become involved. A look at American history shows there are reasons for this. Before the United States gained its independence, much of the North American continent had been colonized by European nations. Native Americans and colonists alike were dragged into European conflicts as Spain, France, and Britain—often at war with each other—fought out their battles on American soil.

In the American Revolution, colonists declared their intention to be free of foreign rule and fought as Americans for the first time, against Britain. After independence, and because of their history as colonists, Americans had a deep-rooted opposition both to the undemocratic policies of European rulers and to their greed for colonies overseas. In 1823, President James Monroe made a declaration to the world. The Monroe Doctrine stated that the U.S. would not tolerate other nations trying to expand their powers or systems of government in America; and that the United States would not involve itself in European foreign conflicts, internal affairs, or colonies.

Although the Monroe Doctrine was not law, it was an important statement of America's attitude to foreign involvement, and it still held during the world wars of the twentieth century. But the world had changed, and it was clear on both occasions that American interests were threatened and so were democracy and freedom.

After World War II, the United States effectively abandoned its isolationist ideals. In 1949, the nation joined with 11 others to form the North Atlantic Treaty Organization (NATO). NATO members regard an attack on any one member as an attack on all of them. Since then, America has become heavily involved in the political affairs of the world. And the United States has intervened with military force in Korea, Vietnam, the Middle East, Africa, Central America, and Eastern Europe.

The War Goes Global

The Axis had secured a frightening grip on Western Europe by early 1941. With arrogance and aggression, Axis forces began to spread out.

Battle of the Atlantic

Because Nazi Germany had lost out in the Battle of Britain, Hitler put more effort into destroying merchant shipping and British naval forces in the Atlantic Ocean. The merchant ships belonged to Allied nations, such as Canada, or to neutral countries, including the United States, and were bringing supplies to the Allies in Europe.

German submarine attacks had begun in April 1940, but now they intensified. The Germans set up bases from which they could send out submarines, or U-boats, to launch torpedo attacks on convoys of merchant ships. These attacks were named the "Battle of the Atlantic" by Prime Minister Winston Churchill, and continued into 1943.

A German submarine, or U-boat, surfaces in the Atlantic Ocean to be caught unawares by an Allied bomber. The Battle of the Atlantic lasted for several years and damaged or sank many merchant ships. The advances in radar and increase in forces later in the war, however, helped the Allies fight back.

Fighting in Africa and the Balkans

In 1940, while Britain and Germany's focus was on the
Battle of Britain and the Battle of the Atlantic, Mussolini
tried to take control in northern Africa. From Italy's base in
Libya, he struck at neighboring Egypt, located in northeastern
Africa at the edge of the Mediterranean Sea. Egypt was an
independent nation, but Britain had a responsibility to protect
it. In September 1940, Italian troops moved into Sidi Barrani,
Egypt. But by February 1941, British troops in the area had
defeated the Italians, capturing more than 130,000 prisoners
and costing Italy more than 10,000 casualties. The British
pushed the Italians west to Benghazi in Libya.

Seeing that the Italians were in trouble, Hitler sent
reinforcements in February 1941. German General Erwin
Rommel took over and pushed most of the British troops
back into Egypt. Some British forces managed to hold a
position at Tobruk, Libya. The German Afrika Korps was
fierce, but the British fought back strongly. The two sides
remained locked in battle throughout 1941 and into 1942.

Mussolini had also set his sights on the countries of the
Balkan Peninsula in southeastern Europe, specifically Greece
and Yugoslavia. In October 1940, Italian troops invaded Greece
through Albania, another Balkan nation, but were driven
back by the Greek army. Greece asked for reinforcements
from Britain, which sent troops. But Hitler then stepped
in. On April 6, 1941, the Germans invaded Greece and
Yugoslavia with their infamous blitzkrieg warfare, crippling
Yugoslavia in 11 days. The Greeks and British held out until
April 23, but in the end were overpowered by the Germans.

> "I have decided to destroy Yugoslavia."
>
> *Adolf Hitler, March 26, 1941, two weeks before invading Yugoslavia*

Germany Invades the Soviet Union

After rapid victories in Western and Eastern Europe, Hitler
set his sights on a former ally. Both Germany and the Soviet
Union had used their non-aggression pact to buy some time
and wage war against weaker nations. But it had been likely
all along that the two would turn against each other because
of their opposing ideals of fascism and communism.

"Only a fool would attack us."

Soviet Foreign Minister Vyacheslav Molotov, June 1941

Germany invaded the Soviet Union on June 22, 1941, in an attack named Operation Barbarossa. Hitler rushed in with the full force of more than 3.5 million German, Finnish, and Rumanian soldiers. His forces penetrated the Soviet Union from the west, along a 2,000-mile (3,200-km) front that ran from the Arctic Ocean south. By November, there were a million Soviet casualties. The Germans had overrun large areas and captured major cities as far east as Moscow and Leningrad.

The Soviets were determined to stand their ground, and fought back in November and December. Fighting dragged on through the winter months, which was a great advantage for the Soviets. The Germans had not expected such a long conflict and were completely unprepared for the harsh winter weather. It slowed them down considerably and the two nations came to a stalemate.

Operation Barbarossa was a critical point in World War II. Except in Britain, every Nazi attempt at domination had succeeded so far. The United States was now faced with an awkward situation. Although the majority of Americans did not support communism, the desire to rid Europe of the Nazis was strong. The United States made the difficult decision in September 1941 to include the Soviet Union in the Lend-Lease program. Britain also lent support to the Soviets. Suddenly, the Soviet Union was on the Allied side.

Churchill and Roosevelt Meet

In August 1941, Churchill and Roosevelt spent three days off the coast of Newfoundland, discussing strategies. At this point in the war, the United States was still officially neutral. Churchill once again asked Roosevelt to join the Allies. And FDR again replied that he would need a specific incident strong enough to convince the American people that entering the war was in the best interest of their nation.

During this meeting, the two men produced a document called the Atlantic Charter. This declaration had eight main points that referred to their vision of the postwar world. Among the points made in the charter was that "all men

The Big Three

During World War II, Allied leaders Franklin D. Roosevelt, Winston Churchill, and Joseph Stalin became known as the "Big Three." Their cooperation with each other was critical to the Allied success in the war.

Winston Churchill (left), Franklin Delano Roosevelt (center), and Joseph Stalin (right) sit together at the Yalta conference in 1945.

The relationship between Churchill and Roosevelt was a close one. They met without Stalin on three formal occasions to discuss strategy. The first time was in August 1941, when the Atlantic Charter was written. The second meeting, the Arcadia conference, took place in December 1941; and the third was in Casablanca, Morocco, in January 1943.

The Soviet leader Joseph Stalin, although an ally, had a very different goal from his Western counterparts. Because of this, there was an underlying tension among the Big Three. Churchill and Roosevelt were faced with keeping Stalin on their side while worrying about his intentions of imposing communist rule in Eastern Europe after the war.

In November 1943, in Tehran, Iran, the three leaders met for the first time. There, it was agreed that an invasion of German-occupied France should be launched from Britain. The second, and last, meeting of the Big Three occurred in Yalta, a city in the Soviet Union, in February 1945. The three leaders, despite their differences, ultimately succeeded in making decisions together that led to an Allied victory in World War II.

in all the lands may live out their lives in freedom from fear and want." Roosevelt hoped the Atlantic Charter would help assure Americans that an alliance with the Soviet Union would not endanger democracy and that the United States would figure prominently in the postwar world.

By December 1941, the United States was doing everything possible to assist the Allies without becoming directly involved in the fighting. Roosevelt's "arsenal of democracy" was sending ships, tanks, aircraft, and other supplies to nations fighting the Axis. The Lend-Lease Act allowed America to continue providing this necessary equipment, even when Allied nations could not afford to purchase them.

Pearl Harbor

The ever-increasing assistance that the United States was giving the Allies was a source of resentment for Japan. In addition to this, the United States was expanding its naval presence in the Pacific Ocean and had taken command of armed forces in the Philippine Islands, a U.S. possession. The Philippines are in the Pacific south of Japan, and all this activity was seen by Japan as a threat to their goal of military control in the Far East. Japan's growing anger toward America was about to explode.

Pearl Harbor, Hawaii, was the largest base for the U.S. Navy's Pacific fleet. On December 7, 1941, Americans stationed at Pearl Harbor were enjoying a normal, peaceful Sunday morning. Some were sitting down to breakfast, some were performing routine duties, and others were still sleeping. Suddenly, without any warning, the quiet was shattered as the Japanese attacked Pearl Harbor. Some of the first strikes targeted rows of American aircraft parked at the airfields. The Japanese arrived fast and low, flying only 50 to 75 feet (15 to 23 m) off the ground. Within minutes, Japan eliminated most of the U.S. air power in Hawaii: 188 aircraft were destroyed and 159 damaged.

Almost simultaneously, the Japanese bombers zeroed in on Battleship Row, where eight American battleships were anchored. The *Arizona* was the first to explode and sink, killing more than 1,100 Americans on board. The *West Virginia* and the *Oklahoma* were also torpedoed and quickly sank. In total, the Japanese put 18 ships out of commission.

> "At 7:55 A.M. wave after wave of those warplanes streamed across the harbor and hurled their deadly missiles upon the unsuspecting battle fleet. . . . So terrific was the noise of the explosions and our own anti-aircraft guns that one could not hear himself speak."
>
> *U.S. Marine Sergeant Roger Emmons, later describing the attack on Pearl Harbor on December 7, 1941*

> "I regret to tell you that very many American lives were lost. . . . No matter how long it may take us to overcome this premeditated invasion, the American people . . . will win."
>
> *President Roosevelt, speaking about the attack on Pearl Harbor, December 8, 1941*

More than 2,400 Americans were killed and 1,178 people were wounded in the attack on Pearl Harbor. The loss of aircraft and battleships paralyzed the U.S. Pacific fleet for several weeks.

America Declares War

The day after the Pearl Harbor attack, on December 8, 1941, President Roosevelt asked Congress to declare war on Japan. Congress immediately approved the request, with only one member voting against going to war. The United States had joined the Allies and entered World War II. The same day, Canada and Britain declared war on Japan.

On December 9, China, which had been under attack by Japan since the early 1930s, also declared war on the Axis. And because of their Tripartite Pact with Japan, Germany and Italy declared war on the United States on December 11. Japan's bombing of Pearl Harbor had sparked a rapid chain of events that turned World War II into a truly global conflict.

A conference between Roosevelt and Churchill took place in Washington, D.C., beginning on December 22, 1941. Now that America had entered the war, critical naval strategies and other military issues needed to be discussed. The Arcadia conference was a long and productive meeting, lasting until January 14, 1942.

One of the most important results of Arcadia was the decision that the Allies should first focus on defeating Germany before expending too much energy and too many resources on the conflict with the Japanese. To buy some time in the Pacific, Britain would strengthen naval and military forces there. In addition, U.S. bombers would be sent to British bases.

The surprise attack on Pearl Harbor, Hawaii, that brought the United States into World War II. A few navy personnel stand helplessly on a small boat as men aboard the ships consumed by flames try to find their way to safety.

"We . . . reached a great measure of agreement on many points, both large and small."

Prime Minister Winston Churchill, about meeting with President Roosevelt in December 1941.

47

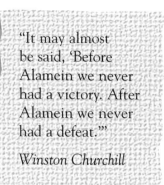

The North African Front

Also at Arcadia, it was decided that America would take part in an invasion of North Africa. In Egypt, where the British and Germans had been fighting since 1940, General Rommel's German forces gained the advantage in June 1942. They seized Tobruk in Libya and drove the British to El Alamein, Egypt. This alarmed the Allies: The Nazis were very close to the Suez Canal, which was an important trade route between Britain and the Middle East, India, and the Far East.

America and Britain immediately sent soldiers and supplies to the North African front. The Allied reinforcements proved too much for the Germans. In early November 1942, under the brilliant leadership of British Field Marshal Bernard Montgomery, the Allies drove the Germans from El Alamein. Thousands of German and Italian soldiers retreated westward across Libya and into Tunisia.

The Tuskegee Airmen

When America entered World War II, there were few African Americans in the armed forces and most were assigned to duties such as cooking and cleaning. The armed forces were segregated, meaning that black and white soldiers did not serve in the same units. But in January 1941, the first all-black squadron of the U.S. Air Force was established. Training took place at the Tuskegee Institute in Alabama and the first pilots qualified in March 1942. In all, 996 men known as the "Tuskegee Airmen" graduated.

The Tuskegee Airmen fought with skill and bravery in World War II. In Italy, they gave cover to the Allied ships approaching the coast and to the soldiers moving on the ground. And they fought enemy aircraft in Austria and throughout Germany. Even though they faced discrimination, the Tuskegee Airmen paved the way for desegregation in the armed forces.

U.S. pilots in Italy in 1944.

Europe, North Africa, and the Middle East by 1942

Legend:
- Axis Nations
- Nations and Areas Controlled by Axis Powers
- Allied Nations Occupied by Axis Powers
- Allied Nations and Nations and Areas Under Allied Control
- Neutral Nations
- Vichy France and Nations Under Vichy Control
- U-Boat Blockade

Operation Torch

Between November 1942 and May 1943, Allied forces continued to push the Axis troops back, eventually forcing them out of North Africa. But it was not an easy or quick victory. Operation Torch began on November 8, 1942, with the arrival of American General Dwight Eisenhower and his troops in Africa. Two of the operation's goals were to convert Vichy troops in French Morocco and Algeria to the Allied side, and to gain a quick victory over the Nazis. The plan, which seemed simple, was for British and American troops to push the Axis from the west and Montgomery's soldiers to push from the east.

However, the American soldiers were inexperienced and suffered great losses in the beginning. Rommel's seasoned

By 1942, the Soviet Union had become a leading Allied power. Other nations had also joined the Allies, but the Axis powers still had Europe in their grip, and many of the Allied nations were occupied by Axis forces.

Two American Generals

Dwight Eisenhower

Dwight D. Eisenhower (1890–1969) and **George Smith Patton (1885–1945)** were two remarkable men who led the fight in World War II. They were both admired and respected for their leadership.

Although Eisenhower had almost 25 years of service in the army before World War II, he had never been in combat. In World War I, he trained soldiers in the United States. During World War II, Eisenhower commanded the American forces in Europe. He was given the highest title in the army, that of army chief of staff. During World War II, Eisenhower led armies in North Africa and then in Italy. Later in the war, Eisenhower was in charge of Operation Overlord and D-Day in France in 1944, and then led the Allies to the Rhine River in Germany in 1945.

Throughout the conflict, Eisenhower displayed a calm and peaceful personality. After the war ended, his ability to be a powerful leader with a cheery disposition won America's heart. He won the 1952 presidential campaign by a landslide, an event that put a Republican in the White House for the first time in 20 years.

General George Patton had a decidedly different personality. Known for his colorful language and fierce bravado, Patton graduated from West Point Military Academy in 1909. During World War I, he led a tank brigade in France. His troops gave Patton the nickname of "Blood and Guts."

George Patton

In World War II, Patton's troops fought fiercely in North Africa, captured Italy in 1943 and 1944, and were essential to the Allied victory in December 1944 at the Battle of the Bulge in Belgium. Patton was brilliant and unique, able simultaneously to take risks with his troops and to protect them. He was passionate about winning and was a master of military strategy. Patton died shortly after the war's end from injuries suffered in a car accident in Germany.

fighters easily outgunned the Americans. And in February 1943, at Kasserine Pass in Tunisia, Allied soldiers were beaten by Rommel's men. This defeat prompted Eisenhower to make a change in command, placing Major General George Patton in charge of those troops.

The Allies did slowly gain control in North Africa. Tobruk was recaptured and Allied soldiers at Kasserine Pass rallied, continuing their advance. Eisenhower's troops drove eastward and Montgomery's troops drove westward, as originally planned. The Germans were squeezed into a tight spot. On May 13, 1943, a quarter of a million Axis troops along the North African front surrendered to the Allies.

The Battle of Stalingrad

Although Axis troops in North Africa had surrendered, the Soviets were still facing the Nazi threat. The Soviet Union

German prisoners of war try to protect themselves against the bitter Soviet winter with coats, blankets, or anything they could find. The Germans were marched through the battered, frozen streets of Stalingrad after their defeat by Soviet forces in early 1943.

and Germany had fought each other through the winter of 1941 and still the fight on Soviet soil continued. By spring 1942, both sides had been reinforced. In June, the Germans captured Sevastapol (see map on page 49). They then headed for Stalingrad and Baku (see map on page 49), which would give them control of the Soviet oil fields.

On September 13, 1942, Axis soldiers stormed into the city of Stalingrad. The Battle of Stalingrad that followed lasted more than four months. From the outset, there was gruesome hand-to-hand combat between Soviet and German forces. The Germans fought through the city until November, with the Soviets battling them all the way.

On November 19, the Soviets began an effort to encircle the largest and most skilled group of German troops. The Germans ferociously held their ground for as long as possible, but the Soviet strategy was effective in the end. More than 200,000 German soldiers lost their lives, and over 450,000 Italian and Rumanian soldiers died fighting with them. By January 1943, the Germans gave up the fight.

The Pearl Harbor Memorial

The attack on Pearl Harbor remains one of the most devastating blows in the history of the United States. In 1958, President Eisenhower gave approval for a memorial to be built to commemorate those who lost their lives on December 7, 1941.

The memorial was designed by Alfred Preis and was dedicated in 1962. It consists of a building that straddles the middle of the destroyed ship *Arizona*. The names of the people who were killed on the ship are engraved inside the memorial. A U.S. flag flies from an original mast of the ship.

In January 1999, the battleship *Missouri* was dedicated as a World War II memorial and placed near the *Arizona*. It was on the decks of the *Missouri* —or "Mighty Mo" as it came to be called—that Japan's foreign minister surrendered on September 2, 1945. The *Missouri* has been restored to its original 1940s condition and serves as a reminder of the time to all who visit Pearl Harbor.

The Home Front

World War II brought a transformation to the United States. Before Pearl Harbor, the majority of Americans were staunch isolationists. By the end of 1941, many had decided to support the war effort. Everyone was affected, and men, women, and children all did their part on the home front.

Economics and Industrialization

The war dramatically changed the status of the American economy. The New Deal had made strides to bring the United States out of the depths of depression. It had altered the economic path of the country and would ultimately affect how long the postwar prosperity lasted. The New Deal also offered a sense of security to many groups, including farmers, industrial workers, employers, and banks.

In 1939, however, Roosevelt told Congress that it was no longer necessary to create new programs and that full recovery would come over time. In fact, World War II brought with it not only recovery but prosperity. To win the war, the Allies needed ships, airplanes, ammunition, weapons, tanks, and other materials of war, such as food and uniforms. America heeded the call even before the attack on Pearl Harbor. Iron, steel, and aluminum production increased greatly, and the rubber industry expanded as new rubber products were manufactured in American factories.

The demand for planes was enormous. In 1942, Roosevelt asked for 60,000 planes to be manufactured, and the next year for 86,000. Both the aircraft and the automobile industry

"Loose lips sink ships."

World War II government slogan warning people to beware of spies

". . . to American production, without which this war would have been lost."

Soviet leader Joseph Stalin, toasting America at the Tehran Conference, 1943

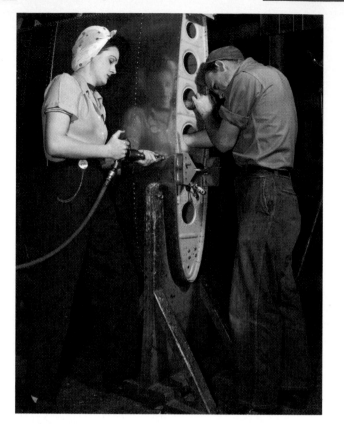

A female defense worker rivets the wing of an airplane at a factory during World War II. The number of aircraft companies expanded rapidly during the war years, and by 1943 there were 40 more aircraft plants than in 1940. During the course of the war, Americans built nearly 300,000 planes.

responded. The automobile factories of Ford, Chrysler, Packard Motor Company, and General Motors began turning out airplane parts instead of automobile parts.

The master shipbuilder Henry Kaiser simplified the way freighters, or cargo ships, were put together and cut building time enormously. In 1941, the first "Liberty" freighter took 355 days to build, but by 1943 Kaiser's shipyard was turning them out in an average time of 41 days. About 2,700 of these cargo vessels, designed to carry war materials to the battlefront, were produced.

Living It Up and Cutting Back

Wartime produced a boom in the economy that resulted in better living standards for many. Farmers' earnings went up dramatically during the war as the price of their produce steadily increased. Many farmers went from living with just basic necessities to enjoying modern conveniences, such as running water, electric stoves, and vacuum cleaners. Wages for workers in manufacturing jobs also increased by about 65 percent.

In general, incomes were up and people were enjoying many items that had not been available to them in the recent past. Americans went to restaurants and movie theaters and bought books, jewelry, and other luxuries that they had been unable to purchase during the Depression. However, these were not always easy to find. The manufacture of private cars was banned in February 1942 to utilize steel and rubber for the war. Production of household appliances such as toasters, washing machines, and refrigerators was also limited.

The supply of goods that Americans wanted could not keep up with the demand. This led to problems with inflation, because prices of goods rose as they became scarce. To fight inflation, the government raised taxes, and prices were set by the Office of Price Administration, established in August 1941.

As part of the war effort, Americans purchased war bonds, which were a way of lending money to the government for war materials. The war bonds were certificates, issued by the government, that promised to repay a person's investment with interest after the war. Buying war bonds gave people a strong feeling of doing their part.

Rationing

During the war, there were many products that were simply not available. To conserve supplies, several staple items were rationed. Under a rationing system, people are allotted only a certain amount of a precious commodity. Items such as sugar, butter, meat, coffee, gasoline, and tires were rationed. People were issued ration books that allowed them to purchase limited amounts of these goods. When their ration vouchers ran out for any particular item, they could not buy the goods even if they had the money to do so.

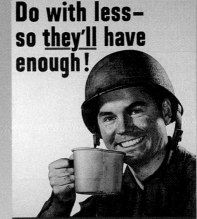

Do with less—so they'll have enough!

RATIONING GIVES YOU YOUR FAIR SHARE

A rationing poster issued during World War II.

Rationing posed some difficulty and led to long waiting lines for scarce items. Some people stashed goods away for their own use, while others bought items on the black market. This was a flourishing, illegal trade of goods, often sold at inflated prices. But many found ways to adapt to the shortage. They repaired worn tires with shoe soles, sweetened foods with corn syrup instead of sugar, and grew their own produce in backyards.

Even children contributed to the war effort. These students in Washington, D.C., are adding to their school's collection of scrap metal.

"Both of us [had] to relate to each other in ways that we never experienced before. Although we had our differences we both learned to work together and talk together."

Black worker Sybil Lewis speaking about a white coworker during World War II

Citizens saved and collected scrap metal to be used for making weapons. Fabric, needed to make hundreds of thousands of uniforms for troops, was also in high demand. The scarcity of fabric changed fashions on the home front. It led to shorter hemlines on women's skirts and the elimination of "extras" such as vests, pant cuffs, and patch pockets on men's suits.

The New Face of the Workforce

Fashion wasn't the only thing undergoing change in America. With a significant percentage of the male workforce overseas, jobs were rapidly filled with groups who had not had such work opportunities in the past. It was one of the most unusual workforces in America's history. African Americans, women, teenagers, the elderly, the disabled, and even prisoners were put to work.

In 1940, racial discrimination was the cause of a severe lack of well-paying jobs for African Americans. But the manpower shortage, coupled with a determination to achieve equal opportunities, was responsible for some advances. On June 25, 1941, the defense industry, which made war supplies, was officially desegregated. This meant that black and white workers labored side by side, a first step toward desegregation in the United States. Between 1942 and 1944, the workforce in the defense industry greatly increased and the number of blacks working in that industry tripled.

More than 6 million women joined the wartime workforce, half of them taking jobs for which they had previously been declared "unsuited." By 1943, nearly a third of the workforce was made up of women. In the aircraft industry alone, there were 360,000 women at work. Women, especially those from minorities, still faced employment discrimination at this time in America, but their skill, talent, and achievements proved them invaluable.

In addition, millions of women worked tirelessly in volunteer positions. They ran Red Cross canteens, drove ambulances, and scanned the skies for enemy planes.

Cities Change as Millions Migrate

During World War II, the populations of cities throughout America swelled. More than 27 million people moved from rural areas and into new jobs in urban areas. America went from a nation plagued by unemployment to one clamoring for more and more workers.

Ships and planes were being produced in mass quantity on the Pacific coast, and the migration to that part of the country mirrored the employment needs there. The populations of San Diego and Burbank in California, Seattle, Washington, and Portland, Oregon, all increased dramatically. Shipyards and plants in Alabama, Illinois, Michigan, and New York also attracted hoards of people.

The need to fill industrial jobs caused a major migration of Southerners to the North. Before World War II, nearly 75 percent of the nation's black population lived south of Pennsylvania and Maryland. Approximately 700,000 blacks moved north to find work during the war.

Native American, Mexican American, and African American women were all involved in the war effort. These women at the first African American Red Cross canteen in Hampton Roads, Virginia, are serving coffee to soldiers preparing to leave for Europe in 1943.

"[I didn't think I should be] selling lipstick when the country was at war. I felt that I was capable of doing some more than that toward the war effort."

Cosmetic clerk Adele Erenberg, who became a defense worker

57

Wartime Entertainment

To relieve some of the tension and anxiety of wartime, show business offered both lighthearted escape and patriotic themes. Movies such as *Casablanca, Mrs. Miniver,* and *For Whom the Bell Tolls* were released. Gregory Peck made his first appearance in a war movie entitled *Days of Glory*. Movies were also used to promote racial tolerance. In 1944, *The Negro Soldier* portrayed positive images of black soldiers and was shown to all troops, as well as in 5,000 public movie theaters.

Bob Hope on his way to entertain troops.

Live theater also attracted both civilians and military personnel. In July 1942, Irving Berlin's musical, *This Is the Army,* opened on Broadway in New York City. In 1943 alone, more than 11 million people saw shows on Broadway. The all-American *Yankee Doodle Dandy* entertained large audiences and another musical, *Oklahoma!,* was performed free more than 40 times for servicemen.

Radio audiences had grown significantly in the 1930s. During the war, droves of people tuned in to listen to war news and to the upbeat music of the Glen Miller Band. Attendance at classical concerts and the opera was up, and dancers who had fled Europe performed ballets with war themes or messages.

Celebrities traveled abroad to spread cheer among the troops. In 1944, movie actress Marlene Dietrich went to Italy and northern Africa to perform for Allied soldiers, and Fred Astaire danced for troops stationed in France. The Andrews Sisters sang for thousands of troops, and comedian Bob Hope probably entertained more soldiers overseas than any other performer.

In some ways, this helped to foster better relations between blacks and whites. Working side by side, many were able to break down prejudices. However, the large black migration sometimes caused problems. Cities could not keep up with the rapidly increasing needs for more schooling, housing, transportation, and sanitation to serve booming populations. In this crowded and often tense atmosphere, clashes between whites and minority groups broke out.

Violence occurred in June 1943, in Detroit, Michigan, a city to which 300,000 white and black Southerners had moved to find work in the war plants. There was a strike at the Packard Motor Company in protest of the promotion of three African American workers. A riot erupted after a fistfight and wild rumors led to white and black mobs of people brutalizing each other. In the course of the riot, 35 people died. Also in June 1943, gangs of white servicemen attacked young Mexican Americans and African Americans on the streets of Los Angeles. Just weeks later, on August 2, another race riot occurred in New York's Harlem, and five people were killed.

Thankfully, these acts of hatred and intolerance were a minor part of the wartime experience on the home front. For the most part, Americans pulled together to support the cause and the troops overseas.

Women in the Armed Forces

Thousands of women joined the military during World War II. In July 1942, the first volunteers began training for the Women's Army Auxiliary Corps. The next year, the unit became an official part of the army and was renamed the Women's Army Corps (WAC). During the course of the war, more than 150,000 women served in the WAC. There were also women in the navy, air force, Marines, and coast guard.

WAC members served both in the United States and overseas. Fewer than 10,000 women remained in the WAC after the war, but the corps was made a permanent part of the army in June 1948. A WAC training center was established in Fort Lee, Virginia, and another opened in 1954 at Fort McClellan, Alabama. In 1976, the first women were admitted into armed forces academies: 119 to West Point Military Academy, 81 to the U.S. Naval Academy, and 157 to the U.S. Air Force Academy.

In 1978, women were officially brought as equals into all branches of the army. In the early 1990s, more than 35,000 women served in Operation Desert Storm during a conflict in the Middle East. Today, there are about 2 million female veterans in the United States and about 14 percent of the U.S. armed forces is made up of women.

The Tide Turns

On the Soviet front, the Germans had been defeated at Stalingrad in January 1943. This defeat was a turning point against Hitler. The German army was no longer an invincible, indestructible menace. It could be beaten.

On to Italy

The first target for Allied troops heading into Italy was the island of Sicily. Patton and Montgomery led approximately 160,000 American, British, and Canadian soldiers onto Sicily on July 10, 1943. They met with some resistance, but for the most part barreled their way across the island. Palermo, the capital of Sicily, fell on July 22.

By August 17, the Italian city of Messina, at the edge of the Strait of Messina, was under Allied control. However, more than 100,000 German and Italian soldiers had already escaped across the strait to the mainland to continue the fight on another front.

During this time, the king of Italy had forced Mussolini to resign as prime minister. Mussolini was arrested and put in prison, but set free in September 1943 by Hitler's forces. Mussolini then organized the Italian Social Republic in northern Italy. Marshal Pietro Badoglio led the new Italian government and began secret peace negotiations with the Allies. Under Badoglio, Italy surrendered to the Allies on September 8, 1943. But within hours, Hitler's wrath resulted in the immediate occupation of Italy.

As Allied troops headed for Salerno on the mainland of Italy, they expected to be met by Italian soldiers now on

Allied soldiers carry one of their wounded comrades from the battlefield in San Vittore, Italy, in 1944. The fight in Italy was grueling for the Allies, as the German troops were highly trained and had better equipment.

their side. Instead, they encountered determined German soldiers not willing to relinquish Italian territory simply because the Italians had surrendered. Although the Allies succeeded in Salerno, the mountainous terrain was difficult and the advance against the Germans was slow.

The Allies in Italy fought a long, hard battle for the next year and a half. The Nazi forces had a good command of the mountains and dug into the rocky hillsides, shooting down on the advancing Allies. But even with heavy losses and weary armies, the Allies persisted in their fight. Additional British and American troops landed at Anzio in January 1944, and on June 4, Allied forces liberated the Italian capital of Rome.

Allied Victory at Sea

The Battle of the Atlantic, meanwhile, was still raging. Radar and sonar (underwater sound detection) technology, used on both sides, was always improving and kept each side alert. In March 1943, the Germans seemed to be gaining an advantage, sinking 43 merchant ships that month. But from May to September 1943, more sophisticated Allied radar resulted in not a single ship lost. Again, the Germans countered with tactics to avoid the radar, but by that time the sheer number of Allied ships made the U-boat attacks ineffective. The Allies claimed victory on the Atlantic.

D-Day and Operation Overlord

It was time to invade Hitler's Europe from the northwest. The Allies decided to launch an invasion on France from Britain across the English Channel. They planned to attack the coastal region of Normandy, choosing five beaches to invade simultaneously. These were sites without good ports where the Germans would be taken by surprise. The Allies planned the attack for months, readying a force of a million soldiers and gathering supplies. They now had overwhelming air superiority over the Axis. The day of the invasion was termed "D-Day."

A view from above of the huge D-Day landings on June 6, 1944. Hundreds of warships arrive on the French beaches, bringing tanks and troops. The airships above are barrage balloons, designed to stop low-flying enemy planes.

Early on June 6, 1944, the attack, called Operation Overlord, was launched under General Eisenhower's command. Paratroopers had started falling from the skies above France at about 2:00 A.M., some of them dropping to their deaths onto the branches of trees or into the cold, choppy water. At 6:30 A.M., troops and tanks began to land. The Allied air attack was ferocious and, at the same time, warships fired on German defenses along the French coast.

There was little resistance at four of the Normandy beaches. But at the fifth beach, Omaha, there were great losses. The American troops that landed there were faced with one of the toughest German outfits. Steep cliffs at Omaha made it hard to climb off the beach and offered shelter to the German soldiers firing down upon American troops. Altogether, 4,649 Americans were killed on D-Day.

After Normandy, the Allied advance in France was split into two main branches. One section, under Field Marshal Montgomery's command, headed for the city of Caen. Under General Patton's command, the other section went east. More Allied troops arrived from Italy. The Germans were weakening and being squeezed out of France. On August 25, 1944, Free French soldiers—who had escaped from France in 1940—together with members of the resistance movement operating inside France, attacked the occupying Germans in Paris and liberated the city. By November, the rapid Allied advance had run the Germans out of France.

Battle of the Bulge

In the winter of 1944 to 1945, the Germans staged a counteroffensive in Belgium, where the Allies had secured the port of Antwerp in November 1944. On December 16, Hitler sent about 250,000 Germans through the Ardennes Forest in Belgium. They were hoping to split the Allied line at a weak point.

The U.S. First Army was in position and the Germans took them by surprise. In addition, Germans had been sent behind Allied lines disguised in American uniforms to cause

> "Within 20 minutes of striking the beach A Company had ceased to be an assault company and had become a forlorn little rescue party bent upon survival and the saving of lives."
>
> *An American soldier recalling the landing on Omaha beach in France, June 1944*

> "History will record this deed [Operation Overlord] as an achievement of the highest order."
>
> *Joseph Stalin to Winston Churchill, June 11, 1944*

The Battle of the Bulge was fought in the freezing Belgian winter of 1944 to 1945. American troops, some in white camouflage, trudge through the deep snow, dragging ammunition sleds to the front line.

"The war is all but over. The God of battles always stands on the side of right when the judgment comes."

General Patton during the Battle of the Bulge, December 1945

confusion. A fierce and chaotic battle took place along an 80-mile (130-km) front and the Germans managed to advance 50 miles (80 km) by December 21. This advance looked like a westward bulge on a map, and the struggle was named "Battle of the Bulge." One airborne division was completely surrounded at Bastogne, an important junction in the area. The Americans bravely defended the town, slowing down the Germans.

The Allied command was quick to send reinforcements. Two American airborne divisions were sent, in addition to three army divisions under Patton. Patton's strategies, backed by the performance of his soldiers, were invaluable. The German advance was halted and the seige at Bastogne broken.

By late January 1945, the Allies had regained the area of the bulge. American casualties numbered 77,000, of which 8,000 were killed and the rest wounded, captured, or missing. The Germans, however, suffered more than 200,000 casualties. It was clear that Hitler was not going to regain the advantage.

The Holocaust

Amidst the general terror of war, the nightmare of the Holocaust unfolded in Europe. The Nazi persecution of Jews and other "enemies of Germany"—such as gypsies, Jehovah's Witnesses, the mentally and physically disabled, homosexuals, and political opponents including priests and nuns—began in 1933.

Kristallnacht, in 1938, marked the start of official violence against Jews. In 1940, Jews began to be forced out of their homes and into ghettoes, which were sectioned-off areas that were overcrowded and insanitary. Food and fuel were scarce and tens of thousands died from starvation, disease, and exposure to the cold.

After Germany invaded parts of the Soviet Union in 1941, a new atrocity began. Nazis would swarm into Soviet towns, rounding up as many Jews and other "enemies of Germany" as they could find. People were stripped of their valuables before being shot and buried in mass graves. More than a million Jews and hundreds of thousands of other victims were killed in this way.

Two of the many thousands of prisoners found by the Allies in concentration camps at the end of the war.

It is hard to imagine that the fate of these innocent people could worsen, but in 1942 it did. For the next three years, until the Allied liberation, Jewish people were forced into concentration camps. The ghettoes were emptied and large numbers were taken from countries under German occupation, including Italy, France, the Netherlands, Belgium, Norway, Hungary, Austria, Poland, and Rumania. Most people on the trains and trucks heading to the camps did not realize that death was near. They were told they were being resettled.

Inside the camps, those who could not work, mainly children and the elderly, were immediately killed. Families were torn apart as herds of people were shuttled into gas chambers they thought were showers. Inside, a lethal gas killed everyone. Those who were not murdered right away labored for the Nazis both inside and outside the camps. Prisoners were starved, treated brutally, and subjected to unbearable living conditions. In all, the Nazis exterminated 6 million Jewish people and about 6 million others.

Soviet Victories

In the Soviet Union, the Germans had held the city of Leningrad under siege for more than two long years. In January 1944, after the victory at Stalingrad, Stalin believed that the Soviets were capable of taking back Leningrad. A surprise attack broke the German seige there.

While the other Allied leaders sought to restore peace, Stalin wanted to impose communist control over those areas he liberated. His aims were made clear during 1944, with Soviet occupations of Rumania in August and Bulgaria in September. In August 1944, a Polish uprising against the Germans broke out. Stalin intentionally held off intervening in Poland until the Germans had eliminated much of the non-communist force there. The Soviet Union then went in and took Warsaw, Poland's capital, in January 1945. One month later, Budapest, Hungary, was in the hands of the Soviets, followed by Vienna, Austria, in April.

Yalta and the Death of Roosevelt

In February 1945, Churchill, Stalin, and Roosevelt met again, this time at Yalta in the Soviet Union. At the Yalta Conference, negotiations were held and agreements made about the war in the Pacific and postwar issues. During the conference, the three leaders pledged their support to all European nations that introduced free and democratic elections after the war.

The Yalta Conference was the last meeting of the Big Three. Roosevelt's health had been getting worse and he was told that he had high blood pressure and heart disease. His doctor advised him to reduce his work schedule, but the busy president carried on with his responsibilities. Roosevelt did not appear well at Yalta, nor at public occasions in Washington, D.C., during March.

Harry S. Truman with Franklin D. Roosevelt in August 1944, eight months before President Roosevelt's death.

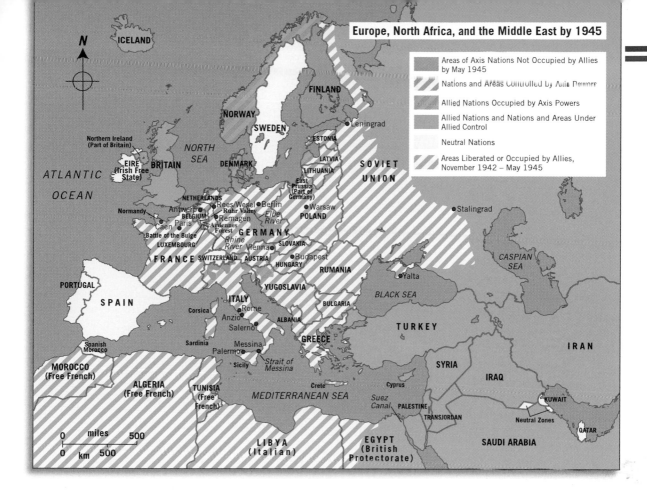

Europe, North Africa, and the Middle East by 1945

Legend:
- Areas of Axis Nations Not Occupied by Allies by May 1945
- Nations and Areas Controlled by Axis Powers
- Allied Nations Occupied by Axis Powers
- Allied Nations and Nations and Areas Under Allied Control
- Neutral Nations
- Areas Liberated or Occupied by Allies, November 1942 – May 1945

The president went home to Warm Springs, Georgia, to recuperate. But on April 12, 1945, while working at his desk, Roosevelt died. The country mourned the loss of one of its greatest presidents. *The New York Times* reported, "Men will thank God on their knees, a hundred years from now, that Franklin D. Roosevelt was in the White House." Vice President Harry S. Truman was sworn into office the same day.

Victory at the Rhine River

Back in Europe, the German capital of Berlin was still the prime target. The Allies had entered Germany itself in October and November 1944. By the end of November, they had taken three German cities. But the Rhine River served to protect the heart of Hitler's Germany. Crossing the Rhine would mean the inevitable defeat of the Germans.

By 1945, the Allied powers were winning in Europe and North Africa. Huge areas that had been held by the Axis were liberated, and the Allies were into Germany.

"There have been few men in all history the equal of the man into whose shoes I am stepping. I pray God I can measure up to the task."

Harry S. Truman, April 13, 1945

In February 1945, Eisenhower staged a massive and critical attack. For four weeks, the Allies battled the Germans and continued to advance. When Hitler realized that the Allies were getting close, he ordered all the bridges on the Rhine River to be blown up. But on March 7, the Allies took the Remagen Bridge before it could be destroyed. On March 23, Patton's men succeeded at crossing the river at yet another spot, between Rees and Wesel. These two Allied breaks on the Rhine were just what was needed.

V-E Day

The Allies headed on through Germany. At the same time, Soviet forces was sweeping westward, nearing Berlin.

Eisenhower's troops concentrated on taking the Ruhr valley. On April 11, they stopped at the Elbe River, a recently designated boundary between Soviet and British-American zones. The American units greeted Soviet soldiers there and all awaited the Soviet invasion of Berlin.

On April 13, 1945, Soviet troops launched their drive into the city, entering it on April 24. For days, the din of

In March 1945, American troops had successfully entered Germany and the huge Soviet attack on Berlin in April shattered the capital city. On April 26, 1945, these victorious Soviet and American soldiers linked arms to walk through the streets of a defeated German town. The Allies had won the battle for Europe.

relentless bombardment filled the air. Although on the brink of defeat, German resistance was incredibly strong. Large parts of Berlin were bombed to rubble by Soviet planes, and corpses littered the streets. And as Berlin fell to the Allies, Adolf Hitler, hidden away in an underground bunker, took his own life.

Elsewhere in Germany, Allied troops were occupying the nation. On May 7, 1945, Germany surrendered. Victory in Europe, or V-E Day, was celebrated the following day.

> "We met like brothers. We had defeated a common enemy. We were united in fighting fascism, and together we had won."
>
> *Soviet soldier Alexandr Silvashko on his meeting with American soldier William Robertson, April 25, 1945*

After the Holocaust

The small percentage of those who survived the Nazi concentration camps had difficulty returning to life as it had been. Homes had been destroyed and anti-Semitism (prejudice against Jews) was common in several areas. After the war, thousands of survivors moved to South Africa, the United States, and Palestine.

Palestine, a region in the Middle East, was chosen for settlement by Jews because they considered it their holy land. Earlier, in the 1920s and 1930s, Jewish people had settled in Palestine and, with British support, hoped to establish a Jewish nation in the region. The Arabs fought against it, and so there was frequent conflict between Palestinian Arabs and Jews. Jewish refugees found prejudice in many of the places they went after World War II, but the worst tension occurred in Palestine.

After World War II, the United Nations voted to split Palestine into an Arab state and a Jewish state. The nation of Israel was established in 1948. Thousands of Jewish refugees poured into the area. The Arabs attacked Israel almost immediately, and there has been turmoil and conflict in the Middle East ever since.

War in the Pacific

While Allied troops were battling in Europe, those sent to the Pacific faced the daunting problem of the Japanese. Japan intended to create a vast empire called the Greater East Asia Co-prosperity Sphere. From December 1941 to March 1942, the Japanese thundered through the Pacific.

The Japanese Gain Control

China had been intimidated and the United States had been attacked at Pearl Harbor in December 1941. The British colony of Hong Kong, as well as the American possessions of Guam and Wake Island, were all conquered within days of Pearl Harbor. The Japanese had also occupied the British colonies of Singapore and Malaya. By March 1942, Rangoon, the capital of Burma, had been invaded. And the Dutch East Indies, which contained vital oil resources, had surrendered. The Japanese had also bombed Darwin, Australia.

On the same day as the attack on Pearl Harbor, Japanese bombers also destroyed more than 235 U.S. planes grounded in the Philippine Islands, an American territory. General Douglas MacArthur, commander of U.S. forces in the Far East, had previously boasted that he could defend the Philippines with the very bombers that became easy targets for the Japanese.

The fighting throughout the Philippines was brutal. The Japanese had succeeded in setting up a naval blockade that prevented reinforcements from being sent to the American and Filipino soldiers. Meanwhile, Japan reinforced its own

70

troops. By May 1942, the Philippines had fallen and Japan had secured more island territory. After a heroic but failed effort to save the Philippines, MacArthur was sent to Australia to command the Pacific forces from there. The Japanese seemed to have the advantage and control of the resources they desired. And Allied morale was low.

The Doolittle Raid and the Battle of the Coral Sea

The Allies had a rough start in the Pacific. But on April 18, 1942, American Lieutenant Colonel James Doolittle led a 16-plane air raid to bomb Tokyo, the capital of Japan. The bombs also hit Yokohama, Kawasaki, and a few other cities, but did not do much physical damage.

However, the incident alarmed Japanese citizens who had been assured that their capital would never be bombed. More importantly, it made a significant impression on Admiral Isoroku Yamamoto, leader of Japan's combined fleet. To him, the Doolittle raid demonstrated the importance of closing up the gap in Japan's defensive line. He also believed that a Japanese attack on the American island of Midway would provoke a battle with the remainder of the U.S. Pacific fleet, giving Yamamoto an opportunity to destroy the fleet and gain control of the Pacific.

But first, the Battle of the Coral Sea was fought. It was entirely waged by the aircraft launched from Japanese and American warships. The five-day battle, which lasted from

American torpedo planes fly over the Coral Sea in May 1942. The Battle of the Coral Sea was the first naval battle in history in which ships did not fire upon each other, or even see each other. Instead, the attacks were all made from aircraft. The plane on the left has just dropped its torpedo, a deadly weapon able to find its way through the water to its target, a Japanese warship.

Japanese Internment Camps

Beginning as early as the 1880s, there were Americans who believed that Asians in the United States were ill-intentioned. In the late 1800s and early 1900s, restrictions were imposed on Japanese and other Asians entering America. State laws, particularly in California, also restricted the rights of Japanese people already on American soil.

A Japanese American child in 1942, waiting to be evacuated from Los Angeles, California, to an internment camp.

The attack on Pearl Harbor in 1941 led more Americans to believe that Japanese Americans might be disloyal to the United States. In February 1942, President Roosevelt signed a document enforcing the removal of Japanese Americans from California, Oregon, Washington, and Arizona. These were said to be areas of military importance where Japanese Americans were a threat to security. Japanese families had to abandon homes and belongings as they were transferred to "relocation camps."

Ten different camps held a total of more than 110,000 Japanese Americans. They were all located in remote desert areas of the West. Living conditions in the camp barracks were stark. Each family's space was tiny and there was no privacy from hundreds of other families crowded into the barracks.

Distinctions were made by the government between issei (those born in Japan) and nisei (those born in America who were U.S. citizens). Eventually, the nisei were allowed to leave the camps to attend college, work, or even join the army. A large number of nisei soldiers fought so bravely and loyally that they were decorated with medals.

By December 1944, when the government announced it was closing the camps, there were still 80,000 Japanese Americans detained. Many returning to their homes discovered losses of property from theft or vandalism. Some, mainly the younger nisei, moved away from the West coast and restarted their lives elsewhere. In 1952, the issei were given the right to obtain U.S. citizenship.

May 3 to 8, 1942, resulted in an Allied victory. Two Japanese fleet carriers sustained serious damage. However, the Japanese succeeded in landing on the tiny island of Tulagi, in the Solomon Islands.

The Battle of Midway

The Japanese then set their sights, along with a large number of warships, on the tiny Midway Island about 1,135 miles (1,800 km) northwest of Pearl Harbor. Midway was an important American patrol base protecting that area of the Pacific. Japan had an overwhelming naval advantage, with its fleet vastly outnumbering that of the United States. But the element of surprise, which Yamamoto had counted on, was gone. Through Project Magic, a decoding system, the Americans were able to decipher Japanese messages involving a complicated battle plan. The Allies gained the upper hand over the confident Japanese and were in position when the attack on Midway was launched.

Admiral Chester Nimitz was the new commander of the Pacific fleet. He managed to have the aircraft carrier *Yorktown*, which had been damaged during the Battle of the Coral Sea, repaired and ready to join the fight at Midway. *Yorktown*, along with two other carriers that the Japanese believed to be out of range, awaited the unsuspecting enemy.

On June 4, 1942, the Japanese began their attack. With the advantage of prior warning, the American planes struck back. Bombers on both sides fought furiously, but the Japanese force was much greater and many American planes were downed. None of the Japanese aircraft carriers was destroyed. But suddenly, at a moment when the Japanese were vulnerable as they readied for the next wave, the Americans unleashed dive-bombers from their aircraft carriers.

"The Americans had avenged Pearl Harbor."

A Japanese official writing about the Battle of Midway

On June 4, 1943, the U.S. aircraft carrier *Yorktown* was hit and set afire by Japanese dive bombers before Japan lost the Battle of Midway. The Allied victory stopped the Japanese advance through the Pacific.

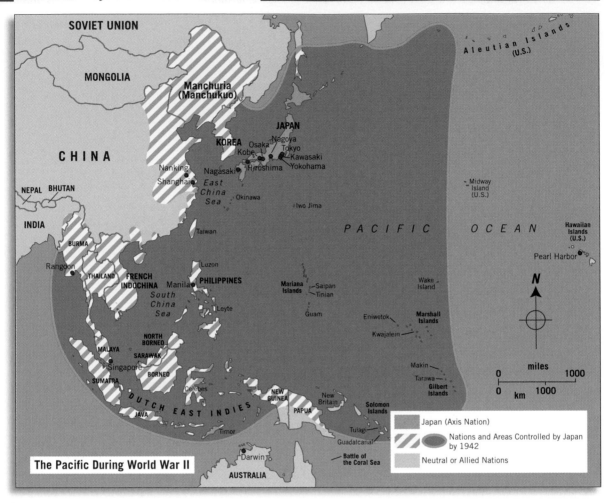

The Pacific During World War II

Japan (Axis Nation)

Nations and Areas Controlled by Japan by 1942

Neutral or Allied Nations

This map shows the extent of Japanese control of the waters, islands, and nations of the Pacific in 1942, before the Allies fought back to gain control. But it was not an easy victory. Many lives were lost and the war in the Pacific was to last another three years.

Within minutes, three Japanese aircraft carriers were destroyed, dealing a strong blow to the Japanese. A fourth carrier, the *Hiryu*, sailed into battle range to offer aid. It managed to attack the *Yorktown* before being attacked itself by American dive-bombers. With four aircraft carriers gone, Yamamoto had to admit defeat. Although some fighting continued, the Japanese withdrew from Midway.

The Battle of Midway was the worst naval defeat in the history of Japan, costing the nation 3,500 lives in addition to the loss of ships and planes. American lives lost totaled 307. The battle was the turning point for the Allies in the Pacific. It marked the end of a retreat and the start of Allied victories.

Guadalcanal

After Midway, the Allies went on the offensive by securing weakly held Japanese islands. This helped cut off supply lines to Japan. The Japanese were building an airstrip on the island of Guadalcanal, in the Solomon Islands, making it an ideal target. About 17,000 American Marines landed on the island on August 7, 1942, catching the enemy off guard.

But on August 9, the Japanese attacked the Allied ships that were providing support to the Marines on land. One Australian and three U.S. cruisers were destroyed. Nearly 2,000 American lives were lost. For the next few months, Japanese and Allied naval forces battled in the waters off Guadalcanal Island.

Meanwhile, the U.S. Marines had taken over the airstrip and completed it for use. For six months, the Marines fought tirelessly in the thick, hot jungles. Both the United States and Japan sent reinforcements, prolonging the conflict, but the Japanese endured a much more significant loss of life, including that of Admiral Yamamoto. On February 7, 1943, Guadalcanal was finally cleared of Japanese forces.

Island Hopping to Victory

Guadalcanal touched off what came to be known as Allied "island hopping" through the Pacific Ocean. In the Gilbert Islands, Americans took Makin and Tarawa at the edge of Japan's defensive line in November 1943. They then advanced toward Kwajalein in the Marshall Islands in February 1944. A strategic Japanese base at Truk was destroyed next. This was followed by an attack on Eniwetok, another of the Marshall Islands, which fell by February 21. And by the end of March 1944, Rabaul, a Japanese air and naval base on the island of New Britain, was isolated.

U.S. Marines medics administer blood plasma to the wounded on the Pacific island of Tarawa in 1944. The new development of blood banks, in which blood could be stored and transported, saved thousands of wounded soldiers during World War II.

> "People of the Philippines, I have returned."
>
> *General Douglas MacArthur, October 20, 1944*

The Marianas Islands of Guam, Saipan, and Tinian were also strategic captures for the Allies under Nimitz's command. Capturing the airfields there would put them in striking range of the Japanese mainland. Tinian was easily taken, but Guam and Saipan did not fall without bloody battles and ruthless fighting. Victory at Saipan came on July 9, Tinian on August 1, and Guam on August 11. And by the end of August 1944, MacArthur and Admiral William Halsey had helped the Australians defend the island of Papua New Guinea. From there, MacArthur readied himself for a return to the Philippines.

The Philippines Are Liberated

On October 20, 1944, MacArthur triumphantly went ashore on the Philippine island of Leyte, followed by 100,000 troops. In contrast, the Japanese had only about 16,000 men in the immediate area. Offshore, American naval forces prepared for battle in Leyte Gulf. Japanese forces opposed them, and the largest battle in naval history was fought from October 23 to 25. But while Japanese resources were running low, the U.S. Navy was enjoying an abundance of new battleships, cruisers, and carriers. Japan suffered many costly hits in the battle in Leyte Gulf, losing nearly its entire fleet.

The land battle took much longer. Reinforcements were sent to the Japanese in an effort to hold onto Leyte. On

The Philippine Islands had fallen to the Japanese in 1942 in spite of General MacArthur's determined efforts to save them. But MacArthur (center) promised to return, and waded ashore at Leyte Island in the Philippines on October 20, 1944, shortly before the huge naval battle in Leyte Gulf.

Douglas MacArthur (1880–1964)

Douglas MacArthur was born in Little Rock, Arkansas, the son of a general who had served in the Civil War and the Spanish–American War. MacArthur attended West Point Military Academy and graduated in 1903. He fought in World War I and then became superintendent at West Point. He rose in the military very quickly and was made chief of staff of the United States Army by Herbert Hoover in 1930.

In July 1941, General MacArthur became commander of the United States' forces in Asia. In 1942, he became Supreme Allied Commander, taking charge of all Allied forces in the Southwest Pacific. MacArthur fought bravely in World War II and was made a five-star general. He was chosen to accept Japan's surrender at the end of the war in the Pacific on September 2, 1945. After the war, MacArthur stayed on in Japan as commander of the occupying forces.

In 1950 and 1951, MacArthur led United Nations forces during the conflict in Korea. He retired from active military service in 1951.

December 6, the Japanese failed in an attempt to secure the American airfield on Leyte, ending the struggle there. But 70,000 Japanese soldiers had already died, as well as 15,500 Americans.

The focus shifted to the island of Luzon in the north, where the Philippine capital of Manila was located. Fighting in Manila was fierce, but the city was liberated by the Allies in February 1945. By the end of March, the Philippines were secure, with the exception of a scattering of independent soldiers determined to try and carry on the fight.

Iwo Jima and Okinawa

Nimitz now concentrated on gaining access to the mainland of Japan, beginning with the outlying islands of Iwo Jima and Okinawa. Iwo Jima had an important airfield and Japanese troops were dug in there. For 73 days, the Allies bombed the island, but there was no surrender. American Marines landed there on February 19, 1945, and struggled through volcanic ash and sand. As they made their way to the top of Mount Suribachi, their combat with the Japanese, often hand-to-hand, was brutal. The Americans planted a U.S. flag on the mountain on February 23. The fighting continued for every inch of the tiny island until the main body of Japanese soldiers was defeated by March 16. More than 20,000 Japanese and 6,000 Americans lost their lives on Iwo Jima.

Okinawa was only 350 miles (560 km) southwest of Japan. In an attempt to avoid some of the gruesome battle conditions that soldiers had faced on Iwo Jima, the pre-landing bombardment of Okinawa was overwhelming. From March 24 to 31, the heaviest concentration of shells to date in the Pacific rained down on the island. The kamikaze technique, first displayed by the Japanese at Leyte, was used in record numbers as Japanese pilots flew on suicide missions directly into American ships. Once on land, American troops easily took the beach on April 1, 1945. But in the southern hills, where most of the battle was fought, a force of more than 70,000 Japanese awaited them.

The battle on Okinawa lasted three months, costing 100,000 Japanese lives including civilians. The U.S. lost 7,613 men. On June 22, 1945, the two Japanese generals took their own lives. Japan's resistance on Okinawa was over.

Hiroshima and Nagasaki

The final step in the plan to defeat Japan was to attack the mainland itself. Six Japanese cities were bombed by air between March and June 1945. Severe Japanese losses were sustained in the cities of Tokyo, Nagoya, Kobe, Yokohama, Osaka, and Kawasaki. Yet the Japanese government showed no signs of surrender. A land invasion was another option, but Allied casualty estimates of such action were staggering: Many believed it could cost up to a million lives. The threat of a Soviet invasion of Japan also loomed.

The war, however, was to end by a different and terrible means. The atomic bomb had been developed in secrecy and tested on July 16, 1945, in New Mexico. It would bring a swift and lethal conclusion to the war, but ordering its use was a very momentous decision as it would cause mass destruction and death.

On July 26, 1945, the Allies delivered an ultimatum to Japan: Surrender or be destroyed. On July 29, Japan rejected the terms of surrender. On August 6, 1945, U.S. Colonel Paul W. Tibbets took off with his crew in a B-29 bomber from Tinian Island in the Marianas. His plane, the *Enola Gay*, accompanied by five other U.S. planes, headed for Hiroshima, a city of about 320,000 people that was also a Japanese military base.

At 8:15 A.M., having reached its target destination, the *Enola Gay* dropped an atomic bomb on Hiroshima. Thousands of people died in the first few seconds. The effects of radiation unleashed by the bomb would kill thousands more within a month. An estimated 140,000 lives were taken by the blast of the single atomic bomb.

Hours after the bomb was dropped, President Truman issued a warning. "If they do not now accept our terms they may expect a rain of ruin from the air, the like of which has never been seen on this earth." There was no response from the Japanese.

On August 9, the Soviet Union attacked the Japanese in Manchuria in a declaration of war. On the same day, the United States dropped a second atomic bomb on the city of Nagasaki, a major Japanese naval base. Approximately 70,000 people were killed in the explosion.

A view of Hiroshima after the atomic bomb was dropped on August 6, 1945. Wood, brick, and even granite buildings melted away from the intense heat. The citizens of Hiroshima, many horribly burned or dying from radiation, found their homes and city destroyed.

Japan Surrenders

Japan agreed to unconditional surrender on August 14, 1945. In a radio broadcast, Japanese Emperor Hirohito announced to his people, "I swallow my own tears and give my sanction to the proposal to accept the Allied proclamation."

On the morning of September 2, 1945, representatives of the Allied nations gathered on board the battleship *Missouri* in Tokyo Bay to watch a Japanese delegation sign the official surrender. During the ceremony, General MacArthur said, "It is my earnest hope and indeed the hope of all mankind that from this solemn occasion a better world shall emerge out of the blood and carnage of the past." World War II was over.

> "The time has come when we must bear the unbearable."
>
> *Emperor Hirohito, August 1945, regarding surrender*

The second atomic bomb of World War II explodes over Nagasaki on August 9, 1945.

The Atomic Bomb and Its Legacy

The bomb that was dropped on Japan was developed by a group of scientists in a U.S. government program known as the Manhattan Project. Many scientists around the country worked on different parts of the project, and secrecy was of the utmost importance.

The Soviet Union had been working on its own project, and in 1949 Stalin's scientists succeeded at creating their own atomic bomb. From the early 1950s, the United States and Soviet Union competed in their work on an even more lethal atomic weapon: the hydrogen bomb. This arms race sparked a worldwide fear of a war involving atomic, or nuclear, weapons.

These weapons have forever changed warfare and the way people think about it. Traditional forms of fighting, although still used, would be useless in the face of powerful nations with the ability to wipe out whole countries. So far, this threat of mass destruction has kept all nations from using nuclear weapons since World War II.

In the Wake of War

The Allies had triumphed and the war was over, but not without the world experiencing the greatest war losses in history. Millions of people, both civilian and military, had died. Much of Europe and Japan, and parts of Southeast Asia and the Pacific Islands, were in ruins. Hundreds of thousands of people were left without homes.

The United Nations

Even before the war had ended, the Allies discussed the postwar world at the conferences in Tehran and Yalta. There were difficult issues to consider: how to handle the Nazis, what reparations could be obtained from the Germans, and how to control the defeated Axis countries. Perhaps most importantly, the Allies believed strongly that a plan needed to be devised in order to avoid such devastating conflicts in the future.

On January 1, 1942, the seed was sown for such a plan when 26 nations had pledged to fight the Axis together in a "Declaration by United Nations." Over the next three years, the Allies discussed creating a world peacekeeping body that would help prevent future conflicts.

In April 1945, delegates from 50 nations met in San Francisco,

Allied citizens and service people all over the world celebrated victory over Japan on V-J Day, August 15, 1945. Crowds, such as this one in New York City, gathered together to rejoice as the news broke of the end of World War II.

California, to create a charter for a new organization called the United Nations (UN). The United Nations would be led by the "Big Five": Britain, China, France, the Soviet Union, and the United States. These nations were assigned permanent seats on the UN's Security Council, which would settle international disputes. Six other nations (later increased to ten) would also hold seats on the Security Council at any given time. All 50 nations would vote in the General Assembly, which was responsible for overall policy. The United Nations charter was signed on June 26 and went into effect on October 24, 1945.

Dealing with Germany

In June 1945, an Allied commission established zones of occupation in Germany. The country was divided into four zones, one each to be held by the United States, the Soviet Union, Great Britain, and France. An international zone, controlled by all four occupiers, was created around Berlin. In addition, Germany lost territory to Poland as the Polish border was moved westward.

Truman, Churchill, and Stalin met at the Potsdam Conference in Germany from July 17 to August 2, 1945. Clement Attlee took Churchill's place on July 28, after his election as the new British prime minister. At Potsdam, decisions were made concerning Germany's future. Stalin demanded that Germany pay $20 billion in reparations to the Soviet Union, but the other Allies argued that ruining the German economy would have the same bad effects as it did after World War I. In the end, economic agreements were made giving the Soviets the right to equipment and materials in Germany rather than reparations in cash. Also at Potsdam, it was agreed to transfer 6.5 million Germans from Hungary, Poland, and Czechoslovakia back to Germany.

Soon after the war, agreements with other Axis nations were made. Peace treaties were drawn up between the Allies and Italy, Bulgaria, Finland, Hungary, and Rumania. Territorial changes were made, and reparations were required.

In Germany, the armed forces and the Nazi party were abolished. And between November 1945 and October 1946, Nazi leaders were tried by the Nuremberg Tribunal, an international court for war crimes. In addition to those sentenced at Nuremberg, Nazi collaborators in other countries were tracked down and tried or killed outright.

Peace with Japan

The atmosphere among Japan and its occupiers was markedly different from that in Germany. American soldiers occupying Germany did not want, and were not allowed, to befriend Germans. But that was not the case in Japan. At first, there was tension because Pearl Harbor was not forgotten and many Americans had a low regard for the Japanese. Nevertheless, a relaxed feeling between Americans and Japanese gradually grew that defied the recent events of war.

The occupation of Japan was led by General MacArthur, who offered several reforms to introduce that nation to democracy. In 1946, he and his staff helped Japan create the Farm Land Reform Act, which ended unfair systems of farm labor and strengthened the farming industry. In 1947, MacArthur's group wrote a constitution that gave rights to the Japanese people, including the right to vote for women.

In addition, the Japanese postwar economy needed rebuilding. U.S. bombing had destroyed a large percentage of Japan's industrial base. Financial aid came from America, in the amount of about $400 million a year. With foreign help and the hard work of its own citizens, Japan quickly rebuilt much of its prewar strength as a productive nation. Remarkably, by 1954, Japan no longer needed financial assistance from the United States.

German military leaders responsible for some of the worst atrocities in history sit in line at the Nuremberg trials of 1945 and 1946. Witnesses and documents revealed unspeakable "crimes against humanity" carried out by Nazis throughout the war. The worst Nazi leaders were sentenced to death and many others were given long jail sentences.

The United States, and most of the other Allied nations, signed a peace treaty with Japan in 1951. Soon after, the Allied occupation of Japan was over.

Helping Europe Recover

Much of Western Europe suffered economically during the war. Transportation systems ceased to function as hundreds

Life After the War

By war's end, there was almost no unemployment in the United States. And farmers, who had suffered greatly during the Great Depression, had gone from poverty to wealth.

The accelerated pace of production during World War II continued once the war was over, but it was applied to civilian needs. Factories that had churned out bullets and machine parts went back to producing the everyday goods that Americans needed. Appliances that had been luxury items before the war, such as air conditioners and televisions, became much more accessible to everyone. By the end of the war, America controlled half of the world's manufacturing and generated more than half of the world's electricity.

Unfortunately, when the war ended, so did most of the newly formed opportunities for women and blacks. Women returned to jobs they had held before the war, such as teaching, office work, or waiting tables. And 3 million women left the workforce altogether when the men returned home from the war. Even so, there were still more working women than before the war, and numbers began to increase again by 1948.

A ship enters New York Harbor in 1945, bringing home troops from Europe.

Education received a boost with the government's GI Bill that provided funds for thousands of returning soldiers, and others, to go to college. And the population boomed, as millions of men returned home to marry and start families.

of roads, bridges, ports, and even trains had been destroyed. Thousands of acres of farmland had been devastated. Without assistance, Europe would have difficulty recovering.

In contrast, the United States had not suffered any crippling effects on the home front and had become incredibly prosperous and productive. The United States lent millions of dollars to European nations through two financial programs, the World Bank and the International Monetary Fund. But by 1947, Europe was heavily in debt and showing little sign of recovery. A better solution was needed.

In June 1947, the European Recovery Program was proposed by U.S. Secretary of State George C. Marshall. The goal of the Marshall Plan, as it came to be called, was to prevent the spread of communism and to offer supplies and machinery, as well as financial aid, to help European nations get back on their feet. The Soviet Union refused to participate. However, the plan went into effect in 1948. Non-communist nations accepted millions of dollars in aid and were able to resume prewar production levels by 1951.

George Marshall (right), whose European Recovery Program sought to help strengthen European nations against the threat of communism, with President Truman in 1947. The program fit well with the Truman Doctrine, which promised military support to countries forcibly taken over by communists.

World Powers Emerge

The Soviet Union, despite severe war losses, and the United States both emerged from the war as world powers. As the Allies had feared, Stalin pursued his goal of imposing communism throughout Europe and Asia. Even before the war ended, his actions quickly solidified that intention. Estonia, Latvia, Lithuania, and parts of Rumania, Finland, Czechoslovakia, and Poland had all been overrun by the Soviet Union. In March 1946, Churchill warned of the "iron curtain" Stalin was drawing between Eastern and Western Europe. He said, "This is certainly not the liberated Europe we fought to build up. Nor is it one which contains the essentials of permanent peace."

"[The Marshall Plan was directed] not against any country or doctrine but against hunger, poverty, desperation, and chaos."

George C. Marshall

"An iron curtain has descended across the Continent."

Winston Churchill, in a speech in Fulton, Missouri, March 1946

Stalin also encouraged communism in Asia by establishing a communist government in North Korea. In 1947, Greece and Turkey were both threatened with communism. That same year, President Truman vowed to help any nation having communism thrust upon it. This policy became known as the Truman Doctrine.

The development of the atomic bomb was a critical turning point in the relationship between the United States and the Soviet Union. An arms race developed as neither nation felt it could afford to be vulnerable to the other. Out of World War II came the next phase: the Cold War. This period of hostility, without actual warfare, between the Soviet Union and the United States would last for nearly 50 years.

Technology Leaps Forward

Many technological advances came out of World War II. Federal dollars invested in scientific research and development went from $74 million in 1940 to $1.6 billion by 1945. In 1941, the government created the Office of Scientific Research and Development. From this, as well as other smaller programs, came achievements that still affect us today.

Technology developed to fight the war had several useful peacetime applications. For example, advances in radar technology served to improve and expand the commercial airplane industry considerably. (The jet engine was also invented during this time, although it was not used by the U.S. military until 1947, nor on commercial flights until 1958.) Improvements in communications developed during World War II became invaluable in everyday use. And computers developed in the early 1940s pioneered a billion-dollar industry.

Medical research was also given much attention during the war. Penicillin, used to fight infection, came into widespread use, as did other improved drugs. The efforts of African American scientist and doctor Charles Drew produced a new way of storing blood. The blood banks he developed are commonplace today and have saved hundreds of thousands of lives. In all, advancements initiated to help fight the war left a legacy that catapulted modern America forward.

Conclusion

During World War II, almost 12.5 million men and women served in the United States armed forces. Of those Americans, about 300,000 lost their lives. It was a high price to pay for freedom.

World War II brought many technological and economic advancements to the United States. Before the war, the nation had suffered a severe economic depression. World War II was the ultimate cure for that depression. The defense industry in America manufactured nearly 300,000 aircraft, more than 2.3 million trucks, 7,000 ships, 600,000 jeeps, 88,000 tanks, and 6.5 million rifles. Most dramatically, it produced atomic bombs. The nation had become a giant world force.

These developments also brought a dark shadow. The future of warfare seemed to lie not on the battlefield but in the cold threat of nuclear destruction. Atomic weaponry, since it ultimately threatened the survival of humankind, had made maintaining peace essential.

Perhaps the most significant outcome of the war was the realization that there was danger in standing alone and more safety in cooperation. The postwar map revealed political changes in Europe and the sweep of the communist Soviet Union westward. In the postwar world, the United States would find it impossible to return to a policy of isolationism. It had become a world power dedicated to securing both democracy and its own interests abroad. Although the years between 1929 and 1945 had been tumultuous, the United States emerged from this period a stronger, more productive, and more modern nation.

Glossary

administration   The managing of public affairs or business, or the group of people who carry out the management.

alliance   An agreement between two or more people, groups, or countries to side together during a conflict. Countries or people with such an agreement become allies.

armistice   An agreement between two or more parties to stop fighting temporarily.

arsenal   A store of weapons and ammunition.

blockade   To cut off an enemy area, for instance by preventing ships and supplies from going into or out of ports.

constitution   The basic plan and principles of a government.

counteroffensive   A return military attack by a force that has just been attacked.

delegate   The person chosen to represent others at a meeting or in making decisions.

democracy   A system in which people are their own authority rather than being ruled over by an unelected leader. In a democratic system, people vote on decisions, or elect representatives to vote for them.

depression   A time when the economy of a country or region goes into a severe decline, resulting in very low production and high unemployment.

desegregation   The elimination or official banning of segregation.

economic   To do with the economy, meaning the production and use of goods and services, and the system of money that is used for the flow of goods and services.

export   To send something abroad to sell or trade. An export is also the thing that is sent, such as steel or manufactured goods.

federal   To do with the central, or national, government of a country rather than the regional, or state, governments.

fortifications   Structures built or made stronger to keep out enemies.

front   The area of conflict or battle line between opposing armies.

inflation   A rise in prices due usually to an increase in the amount of money in circulation when there is no similar increase in the amount of available goods and services.

interest   An extra amount of money paid back by a borrower to a lender of funds.

intervention   Interfering or getting involved in the political affairs of another nation.

isolationism	The policy of staying out of foreign affairs and not entering into alliances with other nations.
labor union	An organization of workers that exists to improve the working conditions of its members and negotiate on their behalf with employers.
legislation	Laws, or the making of laws.
liberal	A political attitude that supports progress and reform in society and the involvement of government in the welfare and civil rights of citizens.
migration	Movement from one place to another in search of a new place to live.
neutral	Not involved in either side of an issue or dispute.
policy	A plan or way of doing things that is decided on, and then used in managing situations, making decisions, or tackling problems.
radar	A system using radio waves to detect and locate objects.
radical	A person who favors extreme political, economic, or social changes or reform.
recession	A time when the economy of a country or region slows down, resulting in businesses cutting back on production and workers losing their jobs.
reform	A change intended to improve conditions.
segregation	The policy of keeping people from different racial or ethnic groups separate, usually with one group having fewer rights than another.
siege	A military operation in which attackers surround their targets and try to force them to surrender by bombarding them or cutting off their supplies.
strategy	The overall plan for dealing with an enemy or a conflict.
tactics	The moves made to try and defeat an enemy.
technology	The knowledge and ability that improves ways of doing practical things. A person performing any task with a tool is using technology.
treaty	An agreement reached between two or more groups or countries after discussion and negotiation.
unconstitutional	An action or law not authorized by the Constitution.
veteran	A person who served for a long time at a job, particularly in the military, or who served on a specific campaign or expedition.
welfare	Assistance given by government programs in the form of money or necessities to help those in need.

Time Line

1919	Treaty of Versailles signed.
1924	Dawes Plan set up to stabilize German economy.
1929	Stock market crashes and Great Depression begins.
1932	Japan takes over Chinese region of Manchuria.
1933	Franklin Delano Roosevelt becomes president.
	Roosevelt's New Deal legislation enacted, creating federal programs including FDIC, FERA, AAA, NRA, and PWA.
	Prohibition ends.
1934	Drought and winds bring "Dust Bowl" years to large area of Midwest.
	Securities and Exchange Commission set up.
1935	Social Security Act passed.
	WPA formed.
	Committee for Industrial Organization founded by AFL.
	Adolf Hitler defies Treaty of Versailles.
1936	Italy conquers Ethiopia.
1937	Japan invades China.
	Memorial Day Massacre.
March 1938	Hitler annexes Austria.
November 9, 1938	*Kristallnacht* in Germany.
August 23, 1939	Hitler and Joseph Stalin sign non-aggression pact.
September 1, 1939	Germany invades Poland and World War II begins.
September 3, 1939	Britain and France declare war on Germany.
November 30, 1939	Soviet Union invades Finland.
April 9, 1940	Germany invades Denmark and Norway.
May 10, 1940	Germany invades Belgium and Netherlands.
June 10, 1940	Italy declares war on France and Great Britain.
June 17, 1940	France falls to Germany.
July 10, 1940	Battle of Britain begins.
September 1940	Japan signs Tripartite Pact with Germany and Italy.
March 1941	Congress passes Lend-Lease Act.
June 22, 1941	Germans invade Soviet Union in Operation Barbarossa.
August 1941	Atlantic Charter drafted in Argentia Bay, off Newfoundland.
December 7, 1941	Japan attacks Pearl Harbor.

December 8, 1941	U.S., Canada, and Great Britain declare war on Japan.
December 9, 1941	China declares war on Axis nations.
December 22, 1941	Arcadia Conference begins in Washington, D.C.
April 18, 1942	Doolittle Raid on Tokyo, Japan.
June 4, 1942	Battle of Midway in Pacific Ocean.
June 21, 1942	Tobruk, Libya, seized by Germany.
May 1942	Women's Army Auxiliary Corps formed.
November 8, 1942	Allies land in Morocco and Algeria in Operation Torch.
February 2, 1943	Soviet victory in Battle of Stalingrad.
May 13, 1943	Axis troops in North Africa surrender.
June–August 1943	Race riots occur in American cities.
September 9, 1943	Allied forces land in Salerno, Italy.
November 1943	Stalin, Churchill, and Roosevelt meet in Tehran, Iran.
June 6, 1944	Allies invade Normandy on D-Day in Operation Overlord.
August 1944–April 1945	Soviet Union invades several nations in Eastern Europe.
August 25, 1944	Paris, France, liberated by Allies.
December 16–21, 1944	Battle of the Bulge.
February 1945	Yalta Conference held in Soviet Union.
February–June 1945	U.S. fights Japan on islands of Iwo Jima and Okinawa, Japan.
March 1945	Allies advance into Germany across Rhine River.
	Philippine Islands liberated by Allies.
April 1945	Allies invade German capital of Berlin.
April 12, 1945	Roosevelt dies and Harry S. Truman becomes president.
April 28, 1945	Benito Mussolini killed.
April or May 1945	Adolf Hitler commits suicide.
May 7, 1945	Germany surrenders to Allies.
July 17, 1945	Potsdam Conference begins in Germany.
August 6, 1945	United States drops atomic bomb on Hiroshima, Japan.
August 9, 1945	United States drops atomic bomb on Nagasaki, Japan.
August 14, 1945	Japan agrees to unconditional surrender to Allies.
October 24, 1945	United Nations established as charter goes into effect.
November 1945	Nuremberg Trials begin in Germany.
1948	Marshall Plan goes into effect.
1951	United States signs peace treaty with Japan.

Further Reading

Backrach, Susan B. *Tell Them We Remember: The Story of the Holocaust with Images from the United States Holocaust Memorial Museum*. New York: Little, Brown & Co., 1994.

Colman, Penny. *Rosie the Riveter: Women Working on the Home Front in World War II*. New York: Crown, 1995.

Lobel, Anita. *No Pretty Pictures: A Child of War*. New York: Greenwillow Books, 1998.

McKissack, Patricia and McKissack, Frederick. *Red-Tail Angels: The Story of the Tuskegee Airmen of World War II*. New York: Walker, 1995.

Nishi, Dennis. *Life During the Great Depression* (Way People Lived Series). San Diego, CA: Lucent Books, 1997.

Steins, Richard. *Allies Against Axis: World War II (1940-1950)*. New York: Twenty-First Century Books, 1995.

Tunnell, Michael O. and George W. Chilcoat. *The Children of Topaz: The Story of a Japanese-American Internment Camp Based on a Classroom Diary*. New York: Holiday House, 1996.

Websites

Voices from the Thirties: Life Histories from the Federal Writers' Project – First-person accounts of American life during the Great Depression as gathered by writers working for the New Deal's Works Project Administration.
http:/www.loc.gov/wpaintro/wpa.home

New Deal Network – An online archive of documents, photographs, essays, articles, and historical material related to the presidency of Franklin D. Roosevelt.
http:/www.newdeal.fri/org

Holocaust Survivors Encyclopedia – Written and spoken first-person accounts, photographs, and an encyclopedia.
http:/www.holocaustsurvivors.org

Bibliography

Ambrose, Stephen E. *Eisenhower*. New York: Simon & Schuster, 1983.

Bailey, Ronald H. *The Home Front: U.S.A.* New York: Time-Life Books, 1977.

Bennett, Lerone, Jr. *Before the Mayflower: A History of Black America*. Chicago, IL: Johnson Publishing Co., 1969.

Brandt, Nat. *Harlem at War: The Black Experience in WWII*. Syracuse, NY: Syracuse University Press, 1996.

Cook, Blanche Wiesen. *Eleanor Roosevelt, Volume 2*. New York: Viking, 1999.

Dryden, Charles W. *A-Train: Memoirs of a Tuskegee Airman*. Tuscaloosa, AL: The University of Alabama Press, 1997.

Hodgson, Godfrey. *People's Century: The Ordinary Men and Women Who Made the Twentieth Century*. New York: Times Books, Random House, 1998.

Keegan, John. *The Second World War*. New York: Penguin Books, 1990.

Kennedy, David M. *Freedom From Fear: The American People in Depression and War, 1929–1945*. New York: Oxford University Press, 1999.

Klingaman, William K. *The Year of the Great Crash*. New York: Harper & Row, 1989.

Leuchtenburg, William E. *New Deal and War: 1933–1945*. New York: Time-Life Books, 1974.

Lowenheim, Francis L., Harold D. Langley, and Manfred Jonas, eds. *Roosevelt and Churchill: Their Secret Wartime Correspondence*. New York: Da Capo Press, 1990.

Maule, Henry. *The Great Battles of World War II*. New York: Galahad Books, 1972.

May, Ernest R. *Boom and Bust: 1917-1932*. New York: Time-Life Books, 1974.

McElvaine, Robert S. *The Great Depression*. New York: Times Books, 1984.

Meltzer, Milton. *The Black Americans: A History in Their Own Words*. New York: Crowell, 1984.

Morris, Richard B. and James Woodress, eds. *Voices from America's Past, Volume 3*. New York: E.P. Dutton & Co., 1963.

Munves, James. *A Short Illustrated History of the United States*. New York: Grosset & Dunlap, 1965.

O'Neill, William L. *A Democracy at War*. New York: Free Press, 1993.

Sevareid, Eric, and editors of Time-Life Books. *History of the Second World War*. New York: Time-Life Books, 1989.

Index